I HAD LUNCH WITH GOD

Gospel Inspirations
for Tough Times

Dear Debbie,

I read a chapter from this booK every night in good times and difficult times.

Please Enjoy!

Love,
Jerry et al

I HAD LUNCH WITH GOD

Gospel Inspirations
for Tough Times

By Kathleen M. Sullivan, Ph.D

+

Corby Books
Notre Dame, Indiana

I Had Lunch With God

Gospel Inspirations
for Tough Times

Copyright 2008 by Kathleen M. Sullivan

10 9 8 7 6 5 4 3 2 1

ISBN 978-0-9776458-5-5

Published by Corby Books
A Division of Corby Publishing
Box 93
Notre Dame, IN 46556
fax: 574 698-7600
email: corbybooks1@aol.com

Manufactured in the United States of America

Preface

IT'S ALL ABOUT THE CONVERSATION. When I sit down to write, I ask the Lord to take a seat in the empty chair. I always need his help – it's just too easy to let my own ego take over. Lord, what comfort do people need? What about those prayers that just don't seem to get answered? So many of us feel the drain of worry – drifting teenagers, sick family members, aging parents, more bills and less money.

This conversation began in February of 2007 when I created pray.nd.edu. For the previous 17 years I had developed enrichment programs for Notre Dame Alumni. Though never complacent, I was comfortable. But 2005 would begin a new era for the Alumni Association and new thinking would direct our course. Change certainly tilted my sails and moved me into unchartered waters. I was asked to oversee a new initiative, the integration of Spirituality and Service for our Notre Dame Alumni and their communities.

Here was my question: Would it be possible to bring the spiritual experience of Notre Dame into people's work space and into their homes? That question eventually led to this book. The prayer site features a weekly music video of a sacred place on campus, a daily prayer, the Gospel of the day, and my reflection on that Gospel. People also send their prayer requests which are remembered at the Grotto every Thursday.

After a few months, people began to write encouraging messages to me. They went something like this: "We like how you use stories – entertaining and a great teaching tool to connect us with the Gospels. We feel like you are speaking to us – personal and real. I have turned to pray.nd.edu as the foundation for my day."

Acknowledgments

To my family – my parents Ed and Jean Thompson, my husband Mike, daughter Christina, to my sisters Mary Keilholtz and Patricia Blake, to my brothers Eddie and Tim Thompson and to my nephew Jonathan Keilholtz – you are the salt of the earth, the inspiration behind so many of these reflections.

To the Executive Director of the Alumni Association, Chuck Lennon, mentor and friend, who passionately believed in the pray.nd.edu website and permitted me to utilize the website for this book.

To all the people who have creatively contributed to pray.nd.edu – Arthur Frericks, Marian Appleton, Fr. Steve Gibson, CSC, Susan Good, Pat Trost, Adam Fairholm, Jack Sacco, Tim O'Neill, Chas Grundy, Robby Maher, Rev. Herb Yost, CSC, Rev. William Simmons, CSC, Steve Hutchison, Christopher Salvador, Matt Klawitter, Christina Sullivan, and Chris Bellairs.

To those who lovingly encouraged me to write this book or guided me through the journey of creating pray.nd.edu – Vicki Skodras, Bob Muenchen, Joe Krug, Marilyn and Ed Fitzgerald, Jim Keegan, Dick Nussbaum, Stella DePaula, Lori Heaton, Mary Rose, Fr. Paul Detsch.

And to my publisher, Jim Langford, who made it happen with his vision, talent, and heart of gold.

In the Moment

ONE DAY A FATHER AND HIS RICH FAMILY took his young son on a trip to the country with the intention of showing him how poor people can be. They spent a day and a night in the farm of a very poor family. When they got back from their trip the father asked his son "What did you learn?" The son answered, "I saw that we have a dog at home, and they have four. We have a pool that reaches to the middle of the garden; they have a creek that has no end. We have imported lamps in the garden; they have the stars. Our patio reaches to the front yard; they have a whole horizon. When the little boy was finishing, his father was speechless. His son added, "Thanks, Dad, for showing me how poor we are!" (author unknown)

As you move through your day, count how many times you stare past the moment – pressing to reach another destination point. Maybe it's wishing a certain meeting would end, maybe it's a particular chore you don't enjoy, maybe it's getting an errand completed, or a workout finished. Maybe it's picking the kids up, getting through their home-work, getting organization into the night activities. If we are not careful, life will become a blur, a routine of black outs, where now is never good enough and tomorrow is simply a repeat of today. We will look only to realize that we have missed the parade and there's no reclaiming its wonder.

The little boy in the story savored the natural gifts of life. He re-ceived their wonderment and filled up on their richness. The child's fulfillment is God's intention for us. When we tighten our grip only on achieving, when we clench our jaws to make time work just for us, we become like the rich, young man - wealthy but hollow. The young man's invitation to follow Jesus resonates with us. While we may not have abundant wealth, we do have abundant minutes. Sadly, the young man turned away from Jesus to preserve his assets. To live joyfully and fully with our Lord, we need to aspire to a rich calling – keep both feet in the minute and enjoy a spirit of renewal.

A Court Scene to Remember

A STORY IS TOLD ABOUT FIORELLO LAGUARDIA, the mayor of New York City during the worst days of the Great Depression. He was nicknamed 'the Little Flower' because he stood only five foot four and always wore a carnation in his lapel. A colorful character, he would take entire orphanages to baseball games. Whenever the New York newspapers were on strike, he would go on the radio and read the Sunday funnies to the kids. One bitterly cold night in January of 1935, the mayor turned up at a night court that served the poorest ward of the city. LaGuardia dismissed the judge for the evening and took over the bench himself. Within a few minutes, a tattered old woman was brought before him, charged with stealing a loaf of bread. She told LaGuardia that her daughter's husband had deserted her, her daughter was sick, and her two grandchildren were starving. But the shopkeeper, from whom the bread was stolen, refused to drop the charges.

LaGuardia sighed. He turned to the woman and said "I've got to punish you. The law makes no exceptions—ten dollars or ten days in jail." But even as he pronounced sentence, the mayor was already reaching into his pocket. He extracted a bill and tossed it into his famous sombrero saying: "Here is the ten dollar fine which I now remit; and furthermore I am going to fine everyone in this courtroom fifty cents for living in a town where a person has to steal bread so that her grandchildren can eat." The following day the newspapers reported that $47.50 was turned over to a bewildered old lady and fifty cents to the red-faced grocery store owner. As for the mayor, he received a standing ovation. (Brennan Manning, *The Ragamuffin Gospel*)

Like LaGuardia, Jesus fulfills the law so love triumphs. "Think not that I have come to abolish the law and the prophets; I have come not to abolish them but to fulfill them." To the devoted Jewish believer, nothing was more sacred than the Law. But Jesus claims that the goal of Scripture is found in him. At his baptism, the Holy Spirit affirms this as the voice of the heavenly Father comes from on high,

"You are my beloved Son, in you I am well pleased" What if each night before we drifted off to sleep, we could hear a similar voice? In time those collective affirmations would form the pinnacle announcement, "Welcome home. In you I am well pleased." Today the Father waits to salute you! How can you team with him to bring a little more kindness, honesty, and appreciation to those who cross your path? Slow down. Don't undervalue the importance of keeping that get-together with a friend, of pausing to ask about the other, or of giving your full attention to those who count on your love.

Which is Easier for You?

EVERYBODY RECOGNIZES THAT Ludwig van Beethoven was a musical genius. But few realize the adversity he had to overcome to achieve greatness. In his twenties, Beethoven began to lose his hearing. This problem haunted him into the middle years of his life, but he kept it a guarded secret. By the time he reached his fifties, Beethoven was completely deaf. But he refused to give up. He was once overheard shouting at the top of his voice, "I will take life by the throat!"

In the Gospel story about the paralyzed man, it was a commitment similar to Beethoven's that inspired the paralytic's friends to find a way to reach Jesus. The paralytic must have been so loved; his friends carried him on his bed finally edging their way to the Lord. Sometimes we are the friend beseeching our Lord to help our loved one. Sometimes we are the paralytic desperate for healing. Which is easier for you? Helping or receiving help? Sometimes we struggle to ask for help. In doing so we limit our ability to get better or to receive a hand up. Why is this? Feelings of unworthiness? A pride that will not reveal vulnerability? If you struggle in this area, realize your stoicism is not strength. Accept the help of another. Take a teaspoon of humility and be grateful for those who rejoice to come through for you.

Has Anyone Seen God Lately?

A COUPLE HAD TWO LITTLE BOYS, ages 8 and 10, who were excessively mischievous. They boys' mother heard that a clergyman in town had been successful in disciplining children, so she asked if he would speak with her boys. The clergyman agreed, but asked to see them individually. The clergyman, a huge man with a booming voice, sat the younger boy down and three times asked in a stern voice, "Where is God?" The boy screamed and bolted from the room, ran directly home and dove into his closet, slamming the door behind him. When his older brother found him in the closet, he asked, "What happened?" The younger brother, gasping for breath, replied, "We are in BIG trouble this time, dude. God is missing - and they think WE did it!" (author unknown)

Sometimes it does seem like God is missing. Maybe we just don't feel that connection. In the Sermon on The Mount, Jesus calls `blessed' those who experience the very opposite: poverty, mourning, hunger, persecution. Could it be that this desert experience is necessary to deepen our pursuit of God? For without it, we would remain static and deaf to his beckoning voice. Can we now allow the Spirit to accomplish God's purposes in us even through unwelcome circumstances? Hold to this guarantee: God can make use of whatever happens. Nothing is irredeemable. It's also true that God's answers our prayers but with baffling unpredictability. Sometimes we just need to remove the blinders and see again with the eyes of faith.

Lighten Up

A TEENAGER HAD JUST GOTTEN HIS DRIVER'S LICENSE. He asked his father, who was a minister, if they could discuss his use of the car. His father said to him, "I'll make a deal with you. You bring your grades up, study the bible a little, and get your hair cut; then we'll talk about it." A month later the boy came back and again asked his father if he could use the car. His father said, "Son, I'm really proud of you. You brought your grades up, studied the bible well, but you didn't get your hair cut!" The young man waited a moment and then replied, "You know dad, I've been thinking about that. Samson had long hair, Moses had long hair, Noah had long hair, and even Jesus had long hair." His father replied gently, "Yes son and they walked everywhere they went."

Laughter. What a good thing! Fun -- what a balm for the soul. It's not uncommon to mark our days by our accomplishments -- with the projects and people in our lives. What about measuring your day by the joy you gave and received? By the number of times you laughed or smiled with another. How often lately have you said, "That was really fun"? Jesus tells us that "the kingdom of God is among you." Lighten up. You have the Father, Son, and Holy Spirit in your camp. Sometimes it's helpful to ask yourself, "If things don't go as I had hoped, what's the worse thing that can happen?" Let's pray for perspective --for a spirit that catches the fun and laughter of the moment. Today don't rush past the laughter for the serious. In the laughter of God, you will be refreshed and directed in powerful ways.

"Poison" that Gives Life

A LONG TIME AGO, a girl named Li-Li got married and went to live with her husband and mother-in-law. In a very short time, Li-Li began to despise her mother-in-law. According to ancient Chinese tradition, Li-Li had to bow to her mother-in-law and obey her every wish. The mother-in-law's bad temper and controlling ways pushed Li-Li to her limits. It was time to get help. Li-Li went to see her father's good friend, Mr. Huang. . Mr. Huang thought for awhile, and finally said, "Li-Li, I will help you solve your problem, but you must listen to me and obey what I tell you." Li-Li said, "Yes, Mr. Huang, I will do whatever you tell me to do."

Together they devised a heinous plot. Explaining the process, Mr. Huang cautioned, "You can't use a quick-acting poison to get rid of your mother-in-law. That would cause people to become suspicious. Therefore, I have given you a number of herbs that will slowly build up poison in her body. Every other day prepare some pork or chicken and put a little of these herbs in her serving. Now, in order to make sure that nobody suspects you when she dies, you must be very careful to act very friendly towards her. She thanked Mr. Huang and hurried home to start her plot of murdering her mother-in-law.

Weeks went by, and months went by, and every other day, Li-Li served the specially treated food to her mother-in-law. She remembered what Mr. Huang had said about avoiding suspicion. She controlled her temper, obeyed her mother-in-law, and treated her like her own mother. After six months had passed, the whole household had changed. Even Li-Li almost never became mad or upset. Her mother-in-law even seemed much kinder and easier to get along with. The mother-in-law's attitude toward Li-Li had changed; she began to love Li-Li like her own daughter.

One day, Li-Li came to see Mr. Huang and asked for his help again. She begged, "Dear Mr. Huang, please help me to keep the poison from killing my mother-in-law! She's changed into such a nice woman, and I love her like my own mother." Mr. Huang smiled and nodded his head. "Li-Li, there's nothing to worry about. I never gave you any poison. The herbs I gave you were vitamins to improve her health. The only poison was in your mind and your attitude toward her, but that has been all washed away by the love which you gave to her." (author unknown)

Maybe there is someone in your life who aggravates you; who doesn't deserve your kindness. Maybe this person contaminates you with negative emotions. You simply don't understand how such a person can rebuke you over and over again; how can this person spew contempt when gratitude should roll off the individual's lips? What do you do? Gandhi tells us "No one can make you feel inferior without your consent." You need to protect yourself. By giving control over to the other, you surrender your joy and you empower the other's weakness. Ask for God's grace to help you to love the other yet to love at a distance if necessary. Once you remove the other's power over you, it's far easier to be compassionate and forgiving. You are no longer dependent on that person. In doing this you can truly abide by the greatest commandments. "You shall love the Lord your God with all your heart, and with all your soul, and with all your mind, and with all your strength." And "you shall love your neighbor as yourself."

Some Kind of Skywalk

A MAGNIFICENT GRAND CANYON SKYWALK allows visitors to stare through a glass floor and be awed by a 4,000 foot chasm. This vantage point is more than twice as high as the world's tallest buildings. At the dedication of the site, a few members of the Hualapai Indian Tribe, who allowed the Grand Canyon Skywalk to be built, hopped up and down on the horseshoe-shaped structure and playfully exclaimed, "I can hear the glass cracking."

Our Lord, fully divine and fully human, is our skywalk between earth and heaven. We can fully trust that he will uphold us; his power emanates from his divinity and from his eternal faithfulness to us. "For the works which the Father has granted me to accomplish, these very works which I am doing, bear me witness that the Father has sent me." Perhaps you need to step out over a daunting chasm. Maybe fear of heights holds you back from the challenge. Maybe you wonder if the bridge will hold; perhaps the glass indeed will start to crack. Remember that our skywalk is secured with eternal strength and eternal love. We can do it. Take a step out in trust. Jesus is both the bridge and our faithful companion, who makes the journey with us, arm in arm.

I Had Lunch With God

A LITTLE BOY WANTED TO MEET GOD. He knew it was a long trip to where God lived so he packed his backpack with Twinkies and a six-pack of root beer. After he had gone about three blocks, he met an old woman and sat next to her. He was about to take a drink from his root beer when he noticed that the old lady looked hungry so he offered her a Twinkie. She gratefully accepted it and smiled at him. Her smile was so pretty that the boy wanted to see it again so he offered her a root beer. Again, she smiled at him. The boy was delighted. They sat there all afternoon eating and smiling – never saying a word. As it grew dark, the boy knew it was time to leave for home. Before he had gone more than a few steps, he turned around, ran back to the old woman and gave her a hug. She gave him her biggest smile ever.

When the boy opened the door to his own house a short time later, his mother was surprised by the look of joy on his face. She asked him, "What did you do today that made you so happy?" He replied, "I had lunch with God. You know what? She has the most beautiful smile I've ever seen!" Meanwhile, the old woman, also radiant with joy, returned to her home. Her son was stunned by the look of peace on her face and asked, "Mother, what did you do today that made you so happy?" She replied, "I ate Twinkies in the park with God. You know, he's much younger than I expected." (author unknown)

We've been told since we were children to see the Lord in others. Sometimes that's hard; sometimes his disguise is too complete for us to recognize him in those we meet.. And perhaps, for the same reason, it's hard for others to see the Lord in us. The smiles that reveal the presence of the Lord come from way down inside; they are prompted by a peace and happiness that only grace can bring. People who have discovered the truth of the Beatitudes are the ones whose smiles we remember and cherish. We too can have lunch with God. We too can have the smiles that enrich the lives of others

More Than Just a $20 Bill

A WELL KNOWN SPEAKER began his seminar by holding up a $20 bill. He asked, "Who would like this $20 bill?" Hands started going up. "I am going to give this $20 to one of you - but first, let me do this." He proceeded to crumple up the 20 dollar bill. He then asked. "Who still wants it?" The hands shot up in the air. "Well," he replied, "what if I do this?" He dropped the money on the ground, grinding it into the floor and then picked it up -- crumpled and dirty. "Now, who still wants it?" Still the hands enthusiastically went into the air. "My friends, you have all learned a very valuable lesson. No matter what I did to the money, you still wanted it because the money did not decrease in value. It is still worth $20. Many times in our lives, we are dropped, crumpled, and ground into the dirt by the decisions we make and the circumstances that come our way. We feel as though we are worthless; but no matter what happened or what will happen, we will never lose our value. The worth of our lives comes, not in what we do or who we know, but in WHO WE ARE." (author unknown)

The Pharisees puffed up their self-worth by grounding people down. In their zeal to win converts, the Pharisees required unnecessary and burdensome rules. Such requirements obscured the more important matters of religion -- love of God and love of neighbor. They led people to Pharisaism rather than to God. Jesus abhorred this mindset that locked people out of the kingdom of heaven. In time we will lose everything – life is a series of letting go. But like that tarnished $20 bill our value remains eternal because of our Lord's eternal love. If today you don't feel particularly lovable or don't feel particularly like loving others, no problem. Ask for our Lord's help and move out in faith – hour by hour. There is genuine truth in the slogan that says, "Smile, God loves you."

Some Things Never Change

A NERVOUS TAXPAYER was unhappily conversing with the IRS auditor who had come to review his records. At one point the auditor exclaimed, "Mr. Carr, we feel it is a great privilege to be allowed to live and work in the USA. As a citizen you have an obligation to pay taxes, and we expect you to eagerly pay them with a smile." Mr. Carr replied, "Thank God. I thought you were going to want cash!" (author unknown)

The paying of taxes has been the albatross of people for ages. In our Lord's day, the tax collector was classified as the very worst of sinners – placed in the same category as harlots, gamblers and thieves. He was considered a moral "leper" - an "untouchable". According to rabbinical teaching, a tax collector was to be excluded from any religious fellowship and could not serve as a witness in a court of law. Any money that might come from him was considered "defiled". Typically the tax collectors sold themselves out to the offers of the Roman authorities.

The tax collector Matthew was different from so many who had received the Lord's mercy. Typically people sought Jesus out – like the paralyzed man whose friends took great pains to get to him. But Jesus came to Matthew; he did not dare to seek Jesus! Matthew probably realized that he had sold his soul for the accumulation of money. Jesus, nonetheless, took the initiative to visit with this notorious sinner. In the midst of Matthew's sinful activity, Jesus chose him.

Our Lord does not wait for the needy to come to Him. "For the Son of Man has come to seek and to save that which was lost." We can take great hope in Matthew's story, for all of us are a Matthew. This day Jesus says to us, "Follow me." You simply need the desire to follow – that's all. Begin anew this day. He can make our road to nowhere a path to everywhere.

Something Magical on 4 West

"BLESSED ARE YOU WHO WEEP NOW, for you will laugh." It's quite a leap of faith to believe that the agony of the soul will give way to the belly laugh of hope. He was known as Johnny B. Once an animated business leader, involved father, dedicated spouse and beloved grandfather. Johnny B now spent his days on 4 West -- the wing specified for Alzheimer patients. To see him sitting in his chair, tapping on his tray, preoccupied with imaginary objects gave the impression that Johnny B was removed from the essence of life. But something magical happened everyday on 4 West. Despite the abundance of loss in Johnny B's life, he connected through his smile -- a smile that brought God's unconditional love to workers, floor mates, family and visitors. Somehow he knew when a loving cheek was pressed against his own; his lips would pucker into a kiss that connected soul to soul. On Sunday, September 9, 2007, Johnny B finally experienced the ultimate belly laugh as he enjoyed the most wondrous, welcome home party.

Like Johnny B, all of us will taste the tears of loss, helplessness and uncertainty. Yet we hold to God's faithfulness -- that laughter will triumph over weeping. We pray for the grace to keep going when the going is tough and to give of ourselves when we'd rather give into our sadness.

Treachery and Taxes

An Italian businessman on his deathbed called his good friend and said, "Luigi, I want you to promise me that when I die you will have my remains cremated." His friend asked, "And what do you want me to do with your ashes?" The businessman said, "Just put them in an envelope and mail them to the IRS...and write on the envelope, 'Now you have everything.'" (author unknown)

The Pharisees were at it again. They question Jesus, "Is it lawful to pay taxes to Caesar, or not?"
Because Judea and Samaria were troublesome areas, the Romans had imposed direct rule on the people and forced a census tax upon them. This taxation caused deep anger and resentment. Many believed this practice was a form of slavery and called for violent resistance. If Jesus said it was right to pay the tax, he would incur the anger of the people; and if he said it was not right, he would be reported to the Romans as a revolutionary.

In the ancient world, coinage was considered the property of the ruler since a coin had the ruler's image on it. Jesus knew that by asking these Pharisees to show him a Roman coin they were already demonstrating their collaboration with the Romans. He only had to say, "Give back to Caesar appropriately." Then he added, "Give back to God what belongs to God," as if to say, "You were made in God's image: you have his image stamped on you, just as this coin has Caesar's image stamped on it. You don't owe your souls to Caesar."

Jesus challenges us to live our faith in the world; not to withdraw; not to give up despite the atrocities we may read about, hear about or even witness. If you find yourself complaining about the world that surrounds you each day, challenge yourself to match each complaint with a positive action that brings a bit more hope, justice, and humor to those within your reach.

Hazardous Opportunity:
Hiring Now

IN DECEMBER 1914, Ernest Shackleton, already a celebrated polar explorer, advertised in a London newspaper, "Men wanted for hazardous journey. Low wages, bitter cold, long months of darkness, safe return doubtful. Honor and recognition in case of success." Five thousand men jumped at the chance to be one of the 26 chosen men to become the first to cross the Antarctica from one side of the continent to another. Ice conditions were unusually harsh, and Shackleton's wooden ship, the Endurance, became trapped in the packed ice. For 10 months, the Endurance drifted, locked within the ice until the pressure crushed the ship. With meager resources Shackleton and his men were stranded on the ice floes. Eventually they sailed three, small lifeboats to Elephant Island -- but the uninhabited island provided no hope of rescue. Recognizing the severity of the physical and mental strains on his men, Shackleton and five others made a drastic effort to find help. In a 22-foot lifeboat they accomplished the impossible -- surviving a 17-day, 800-mile journey through the world's worst seas to South Georgia Island. The men, however, landed on an uninhabited part of the island.

Their last hope was to cross 26 miles of mountains and glaciers, considered impassable, to reach the whaling station on the other side. Starved, frostbitten and wearing rags, Shackleton and two others successfully made the trek. In August 1916, 21 months after the initial departure of the Endurance, Shackleton himself returned to rescue the men on Elephant Island. Although they'd withstood the most incredible hardship and privation, not one member of the 26-man crew was lost.

Why would those 26 men take on such horrendous conditions -- especially since Shackleton so bluntly stated the stark conditions? Perhaps the thrill of adventure? Perhaps the conquest of the impossible?

Maybe for the honor? In many ways Jesus provides a similar warning to his followers -- the journey will be brutally harsh and all may be lost. "But not a hair of your head will perish. By your endurance you will gain your souls." Every part of who we are is infinitely, eternally valued by our God. This day be comforted and uplifted. Remember that the endurance of faith is the one place for ultimate confidence -- not that we will be kept from suffering but that our lives will be held eternally in the heart of God.

Motivation Determines Merit

"I AM NOT SURE EXACTLY what heaven will be like, but I do know that when we die and it comes time for God to judge us, he will NOT ask how many good things have you done in your life? Rather he will ask how much LOVE did you put into what you did?"- Mother Teresa

Jesus reminds his critics that his behavior is not motivated by a self-serving ambition; rather his glory comes from listening to his Father. Mother Teresa cautions us to be clear about our motivation; good deeds that originate from selfish intentions miss the essence of Christ's call to serve. Those we help simply become objects to further our own gain. Ask our Lord's spirit to be the driving motivation in your life. Today slowly pray the words of St. Ignatius: "Take, Lord, and receive all my liberty, my memory, my understanding, and my entire will, all that I have and possess. Thou hast given all to me. To Thee, O Lord, I return it. All is Thine, dispose of it wholly according to Thy will. Give me Thy love and Thy grace, for this is sufficient for me."

Expect It and Sidestep It

WINSTON CHURCHILL EXEMPLIFIED integrity and respect in the face of opposition. During his last year in office, he attended an official ceremony. Several rows behind him two gentlemen began whispering. "That's Winston Churchill. They say he is getting senile. They say he should step aside and leave the running of the nation to more dynamic and capable men." When the ceremony was over, Churchill turned to the men and said, "Gentlemen, they also say he is deaf!" (Barbara Hatcher, *Vital Speeches*)

No one is spared the sting of unwarranted criticism. Certainly not Jesus. He had called upon his Father to drive out Satan, who had muted the voice of a man in the neighborhood. Jesus had brought optimal healing -- sanity had been restored, spiritual wholeness delivered, and human communication enhanced. It should have been a magnificent moment of gratitude and reverence. Instead malicious accusations filtered through the crowd. Our Lord could not control what other's thought of him; however, he could control his choice to follow the path of servant leadership.

When you find yourself unfairly criticized for motivations that clearly do not represent your actions, ask the Lord to protect you from the stress and anger that can accompany such treatment. Like Jesus, you cannot control how others treat you. But you have total power over doing the right thing. Therein lies your refuge from the slanderous comments of others.

"Gabriel, Come Back in a Month."

A MAN IS TALKING TO GOD. The man asks God how much a million years is to him. God says that it's a second. Then he asks how much a million dollars is to him God says it's a penny. So the man asked, "God, can I have a penny?" And God replied, "Just a second." (author unknown)

God's timing for Gabriel's appearance to Mary leaves something to be desired. Now on one hand, Mary's "yes" to the angel Gabriel seems glamorous. The angel singles Mary out as God's favorite. She will be immortalized -- the one to bring forth "the Son of the Most High," who will "reign over the house of Jacob." Mary can celebrate her pregnancy with her relative Elizabeth as they discuss their one of a kind sons. But the reality of Mary's "yes" demanded incredible trust and sacrifice. She knew that the public might ostracize her for life; it was quite likely that the village would even stone her to death. We could understand Mary asking for more time before giving Gabriel an answer. "Gabriel, come back in a month, and I'll have a better idea how I feel about the Most High overshadowing me." Mary, however, teaches us the essence of trust. To trust God only when we have all the facts and when everything seems logical requires no trust. Instead Mary reminds us that our hearts may be fearful; we may not know what awaits us on the next corner. Let us join our voice to Mary's and sincerely pray, " May it be done to me according to your word."

Now I Get It!

ELIZABETH ELLIOT, in her book *Let Me Be a Woman,* records the story of Gladys Aylward who seemed unable to accept the looks God had given her. Ms. Aylward told how when she was a child she had two great sorrows. One, that while all her friends had beautiful golden hair, hers was black. The other, that while her friends were still growing, she had stopped. She was about four feet ten inches tall. But when at last she reached the country to which God had called her to be a missionary, she stood on the wharf in Shanghai and looked around at the people to whom He had called her. "Every single one of them" she said, "had black hair. And every one of them had stopped growing when I did." She was able to look to God and exclaim, "Lord God, You know what You're doing!"

Jesus tells us to "Let your light shine before men, that they may see your good deeds and praise your Father in heaven." No one is excluded from this opportunity. God has given a mission unique to each of us - a reason for life and living. He has bestowed a talent unique to each of us and suited to our mission. We have been given the freedom to choose our own path and our own response - to decide whether and how to pursue our mission. And lastly, our Lord has given us a conscience and grace to choose correctly. Today let us ask God the following: God, help me to know what you want from me. Help me to do what you want of me. And help me to do it well enough to satisfy and honor you. (Contributed by Tim Sheehan)

Amber Alert!

WHAT WOULD YOU DO if your child was lost for three days on purpose! After the wondrous conception in the womb of Mary, the glorious Birth, the Wise men and the journey to Egypt to protect Jesus -- and now He was lost! Was their son in pain somewhere? Had someone taken him against his will? Surely he would have told one of his relatives if he wanted to remain behind? Time passed -- only a sickness of heart moved time forward -- three days of riveting anxiety crowded the parents' thoughts. As they rushed through the temple, there he was -- engaging the teachers with his wisdom and posing astute questions. "Son, why have you treated us so?" Jesus is surprised that his parents are concerned about him. Didn't they get it? So he explains and makes no apology. Mary and Joseph are simply baffled by their son's words. But their boy returns with his parents -- a loving son who grows up obedient to them.

Are you anxious this day about your children? Do you struggle to understand how they think and feel? Do you fear for their health; what about their friends; the decisions they are making; do you feel rejected and forgotten? You are not alone. Mary and Joseph stand with you in your pain and apprehension. Call on them for help; they truly understand.

"Jesus, We Need to Talk"

DO YOU THINK MARY ever had a conversation with Jesus about the death of his cousin, John the Baptist? Mary might have asked, "Son, wasn't there anything you could have done to save your poor cousin's life -- at least you could have spared him such a gruesome death. Jesus, I feel awful for his followers. How traumatic to bury the remains of John's body. Help me understand, son, why you let all of this happen." Yet Mary understood that John's death was a precursor to her son's horrific fate. Sometimes we call out to Mary about the inconceivable hurt, tragedy, loss in our own lives. We don't understand the why for the suffering. How bizarre that John the Baptist would suffer such a hideous death just to placate Herod's selfish, vengeful wife. It seems almost a travesty of John's life.

Yet we hold to our Lord's promise. Nothing will separate us from his love. While we are vulnerable, we cling to his life preserving love that never abandons us -- despite the surface reality. Though we don't understand why we must endure suffering, our faith assures us that suffering and death will not have the last word. Somehow through it all we will arrive at a deeper understanding of our life's purpose. We will find a way through because we will keep our eyes fixed on "The Way."

Sticks and Stones

"NEVER LET ANOTHER PERSON'S emotional weakness pull you down. Because then you give away your energy and empower their weakness." Stephen Covey

Jesus had come home to Nazareth. At the synagogue, he read from the scroll of the prophet Isaiah and sat down to preach. His words so infuriated the Jewish leaders that "they got up, drove him out of town, and led him to the brow of the hill on which their town was built, so that they might hurl him off the cliff." Why the drastic response? Jesus read two passages where God had reached out and blessed non-Jews before taking care of the chosen people in Israel. Jesus draws a parallel to his contemporaries. This insinuation brings on the violent response. Jesus understood that the frenzied behavior accelerated from the crowd's insecurity -- they wanted to believe that God loved only them -- the perfect ones. Jesus could see through their needy, insecure veneer. Instead of pushing back, Jesus moves away.

Too often we allow someone's emotional immaturity to control our well being. Do you know someone who really irritates you? Perhaps their cocky demeanor, their aloof bearing, their condescending presence moves your blood pressure up a few notches. How can you sidestep such negative energy -- not give such behavior a power over you? Why was Jesus able to remain undaunted by the men's searing words? Because Jesus was confident -- he believed totally in his mission. If the people of Nazareth did not like him or show him respect -- so be it. His Father loved and respected him. In the coming week, take the following pledge when another's demeanor begins to tug at your serenity: "If I'm true to myself, true to my God, I will give no one permission to deplete my spirit --a spirit needed to bring good to this day!"

Now That's Authority!

TWO BATTLESHIPS ASSIGNED TO the training squadron had been at sea on maneuvers in heavy weather for several days. The visibility was poor with patchy fog, so the captain remained on the bridge keeping an eye on all activities. Shortly after dark, the lookout on the wing reported, "Light, bearing on the starboard bow." The captain called out, "Is it steady or moving astern?" The lookout replied, "Steady, Captain," which meant the ship was on a dangerous collision course with the other vehicle. The captain then called to the signalman, "Signal that ship: 'We are on a collision course, advise you change course twenty degrees.'" Back came the signal, "Advisable for you to change course twenty degrees." The captain said, "Send: 'I'm a captain, change course twenty degrees.'" The reply came, "I'm a seaman second-class. You had better change course twenty degrees." By that time the captain was furious. He spat out, "Send: 'I'm a battleship. Change course twenty degrees.'" Back came the flashing light, "I'm a lighthouse." *(U.S. Navel Institute Proceedings)*

A lesson was learned that day about true authority. Did you ever wonder what it was like to hear the authority in Jesus' voice when he preached? Truth without cynicism. Certitude without arrogance. Sincerity without slogans. People experienced Jesus' power precisely because he did not seek it. His authority resonated because he acted out of compassion while setting clear expectations for his followers. Remember when Jesus heals the man possessed of a demon? Our Lord never doubts his power. Nor is he tempted to excuse the demon because it tries to appease our Lord by acknowledging the divinity of Jesus. Jesus has one mission. He must bring peace to the possessed man. On our own we cannot speak with an authority that is sturdy in its motive. We cannot sustain our fidelity to do right when loss threatens our personal and financial security. The good news – we aren't expected to do this on our own. Surrender your day to him. Gather support from someone who loves you. Trust in God. Believe in yourself. And genuine authority will be yours!

The Home That Has Never Known Sorrow

THERE IS AN OLD CHINESE TALE about a woman whose only son died. In her grief, she went to the holy man and asked, "What prayers, what magical incantations do you have to bring my son back to life?" Instead of sending her away or reasoning with her, he said to her, "Fetch me a mustard seed from a home that has never known sorrow. We will use it to drive the sorrow out of your life." At first she came to a splendid mansion, knocked at the door, and said, "I am looking for a home that has never known sorrow. They told her, "You've certainly come to the wrong place," and began to describe all the tragic things that recently had befallen them. The woman said to herself, "Who is better able to help these poor, unfortunate people than I, who have had misfortune of my own?" She stayed to comfort them, and then went on in search of a home that had never known sorrow. But wherever she turned, in hotels and in other places, she found one tale after another of sadness and misfortune. The woman became so involved in helping others cope with their sorrows that she eventually let go of her own. (author unknown)

Frequently we wonder "why do I have to suffer?" The meaning of life becomes clearer when we realize that we find purpose when our search leads us from why to whom. Suffering, especially chronic physical sickness, deep emotional pain, and death itself, causes a personal crisis that forces us to go deep into ourselves. We ask those questions that are most fundamental to our human existence. Jesus tells us that "Whoever does not carry his own cross and come after me cannot be my disciple" Our personal cross, which cannot be transferred to anyone else, is an essential aspect of our walk with the Lord Jesus. By turning our sorrow into our servant, we find a little more comfort, a little more hope and even the easing up of our own cross.

Get Real

BILLY BOB AND JETHRO decide to go ice fishing. After arriving at the lake early in the morning, they cut two holes in the lake and drop their lines in the water. After fishing for a few hours, Billy Bob has caught dozens of fish while Jethro hasn't even gotten a bite. Jethro asks, "Billy Bob, what's your secret?" Billy Bob answers, "Mmu motta meep da mmrms mmrm." Jethro asks, "What did you say?" Billy Bob answers, "Mmu motta meep da mmrms mmrm." Jethro again asks, "What?" Billy Bob spits into his hand and says, "You gotta keep the worms warm!" (author unknown)

In the Gospel accounts we meet Simon who also knows what it's like to try and try and not get the catch he deserves. Imagine Simon's gut feeling when Jesus tells him to throw the net one more time into the lake. "You've got to be kidding. I spent all night trying every trick of the trade -- and you think just because you tell me to try again the fish will just jump into those nets. Get real!" But Simon obeys. And a super abundant catch results. Simon is overwhelmed by it all. Deluged in feelings of unworthiness, he asks the Lord to leave him. But Jesus answers, "Do not be afraid; from now on you will be catching people."

Perhaps at times we, too, feel the discouragement of the lonely fisherman -- all out effort and little to show for it. Maybe with our kids, our spouse, in our work, through a sickness, maybe with a special project -- anything that has received our passionate dedication. But keep the net in the water. Our Lord wants us to have abundant joy. Keep listening to him. Perhaps like Simon opportunity has visited you --opportunity that might be but a seed of greater possibility. Keep your thinking big. Jesus says to you, "Be not afraid." Stay close to him and develop that opportunity day by day. Remember your playing small does not serve the world.

God's Heart the First to Break

"Do not weep," Jesus says to a distraught mother. The woman's husband had died leaving her totally dependent on her son. Now her boy was gone. During Jesus' time a woman's identity was in her role as a wife and mother. Now she had no identity, and no way to support herself. The Lord, however, restores the woman's future. He speaks to the widow's dead son, "Young man, I say to you, rise!" The Lord is compassionate not because of our accomplishment, our goodness, or even our faith. The woman's faith is never mentioned. Did she follow Jesus before or after this miracle? We don't know. Bottom line - the Lord's compassion extends to us simply because the Lord is compassionate.

In December 1982, a young man of twenty-one years, was killed in an automobile accident. Soon afterwards a woman spoke to the father, trying to comfort him: "I just don't understand God's will." Burdened with grief the father spoke rather harshly to her: "I'll say you don't understand God's will, Judy. Do you think it was the will of God that Marc never fixed that lousy windshield wiper -- that Marc was probably driving too fast in such a storm -- that Marc had probably had too much to drink? My own consolation, Judy, lies in knowing that it was not the will of God that Marc died — but that when the waves closed in over the sinking car, God's heart was the first of all hearts to break."

This father understood the Lord's compassion. Certainly this dad longed for a miracle that would save his son. But God doesn't give us a magic wand that shields us from life's suffering. The Lord, however, does embrace us with his compassion and therein we trust that "In life and in death we belong to God."

The Million Dollar Life Style

AN AMERICAN INVESTMENT BANKER watches a simple Mexican fisherman count the several large yellow fin tuna in his boat. The American compliments the Mexican on the quality of his fish and asks how long it took to catch them. The Mexican replies, "Only a little while." The American then asks, "Why didn't you stay out longer and catch more fish?" The Mexican answers, "With this I have more than enough to support my family's needs." The American then asked, "But what do you do with the rest of your time?" The Mexican fisherman explains, "I sleep late, fish a little, play with my children, take siesta with my wife, Maria, stroll into the village each evening where I sip wine and play guitar with my amigos, I have a full and busy life." The American scoffed, "I am a Harvard MBA and could help you. You should spend more time fishing; and with the proceeds, buy a bigger boat: With the proceeds from the bigger boat you could buy several boats. Eventually you would need to leave this small coastal fishing village and move to Mexico City, then Los Angeles and eventually New York where you will run your ever-expanding enterprise." The Mexican fisherman asked, "But, how long will this all take?" To which the American replied, "15 to 20 years. In that time you will make millions." Then what?" inquired the Mexican. "Then you would retire. "You mean", asked the Mexican, "then I could move to a small coastal fishing village where I would sleep late, fish a little, play with my kids, take siesta with my wife, stroll to the village in the evenings where I could sip wine and play my guitar with my amigos?"

It is so easy to lose our way. So easy to sacrifice what really matters for those empty moments. When this happens, we find ourselves living for the next moment; we miss the everyday miracle because our eyes are cast down the road. Jesus tries to explain this to Lazarus' sister. "Martha, Martha, you are worried and distracted by many things; there is need of only one thing. Mary has chosen the better part, which will not be taken away from her." So well intentioned --

but Martha chooses chores over companionship with Christ. There are ample Christ moments waiting for you today. Is it the landscape you drive by or the view from your home or office? Is it a child who delights in your presence? Maybe it's a hug from a spouse? Perhaps a meaningful project that celebrates your gifts. Could it be watching your kids practice a sport? Or maybe it's the wag of your dog's tail. Your entire life has lead you to these Christ moments. Seize them!

To Please Everyone is to Please No One

AN OLD MAN, A BOY AND A DONKEY were going to town. The boy rode on the donkey and the old man walked. As they went along they passed some people who remarked it was a shame the old man was walking and the boy was riding. The man and the boy thought maybe the critics were right, so they changed positions. Later, they passed some people that remarked, "What a shame, he makes that little boy walk." They then decided they both would walk! Soon they passed some more people who thought they were stupid to walk when they had a decent donkey to ride. So, they both rode the donkey. Now they passed some people that shamed them by saying how awful to put such a load on a poor donkey. The boy and the man said they were probably right, so they decide to carry the donkey. As they crossed the bridge, they lost their grip on the animal and it fell into the river and drowned.

The moral of the story? If you try to please everyone, you please no one. You stand for nothing. Sometimes we find ourselves timid about our loyalty to the Lord. Maybe we don't want to offend; maybe we don't want to appear "old fashioned." Perhaps we fear appearing narrow – out of sync with an eclectic faith. Jesus makes it clear: "Whoever is not with me is against me, and whoever does not gather with me scatters". Throughout this day, there will be opportunities to be loyal to our Lord – to stand for him without embarrassment or apology. He expects this of us. Pray for His Spirit to fortify your courage and conviction.

Under Oath

DAVID CASSTEVENS of the *Dallas Morning News* tells a story about Frank Szymanski, a Notre Dame center in the 1940s, who had been called as a witness in a civil suit at South Bend. "Are you on the Notre Dame football team this year?" the judge asked. "Yes, Your Honor." "What position?" "Center, Your Honor." "How good a center?" Szymanski squirmed in his seat, but said firmly: "Sir, I'm the best center Notre Dame has ever had." Coach Frank Leahy, who was in the courtroom, was surprised. Szymanski always had been modest and unassuming. So when the proceedings were over, he took Szymanski aside and asked why he had made such a statement. Szymanski blushed. "I hated to do it, Coach," he said. "But, after all, I was under oath." *(Chicken Soup for the Soul)*

Like Frank Szymanski, we, too are under oath. Our Lord expects us to live our life free from pretense -- to avoid the insidious lure of hypocrisy.This pressure to impress people (as if they were more important than God), to make out to others that we are more than we are, to pretend to others that we are different from what we are -- can be truly enormous. When we 'act out life' instead of living it, when we lose touch with the importance of integrity and reality, then we almost always diminish our leadership. How do we avoid the hypocrisy trap? Woe to you Pharisees! For you love to have the seat of honor in the synagogues and to be greeted with respect in the marketplaces.

Here are few suggestions for today. Dig down low and acknowledge your sinfulness and that your life is embraced by a gracious and loving God. Be aware of the small tendencies in your behavior that move you down that path of hypocrisy. Be watchful of behaving like the Pharisees who "love to have the seat of honor in the synagogues and to be greeted with respect in the marketplaces." Remember to keep your focus on service not on status!

Stand Up and Don't Go It Alone

TWO FRIENDS WALKED TO A NEWSSTAND where one of them bought a paper. With newspaper in hand, the man thanked the owner politely. The owner, however, did not even acknowledge the expression of gratitude. "A sullen fellow, isn't he?" commented the other friend. "Oh, he's that way every night," shrugged the man. "Then why do you continue being so polite?" asked his friend. The man answered, "Why should I let him determine how I'm going to act?" (author unknown)

Jesus certainly would not allow the Pharisees to determine how he would act. He refused to play their game. On one occasion, a woman with a physical condition that made her unable to stand, asks our Lord to cure her. Jesus could have observed the inane law of the Pharisees and waited until after the Sabbath to cure the woman. But he refuses. Jesus will not reinforce their laws that stifle the well-being of so many. Instead Jesus uses the Pharisees' logic against them and humbles these leaders before the crowd. This Jesus from the insignificant town of Galilee was attracting all the attention and bruising their egos. They would try to twist his compassionate outreach into an infraction against God. But Jesus stands up to the men and brings relief to the woman of long suffering.

Today there may be a reason for us to stand up -- to have the guts to risk popularity and the affirmation of those who evaluate us. Don't go it alone. First pray for those you must confront. Pray to His Spirit to give you the words and confidence. Stand strong.

Change Starts Within

It's NOT UNCOMMON to want to change someone – our spouse, our boss, our kids, maybe a neighbor, a parent, sibling or friend. Trying to change the other can be frustrating and even impossible. The following lesson gets to the root solution for our unrest. "When I was a young man, I wanted to change the world. I found it was difficult to change the world, so I tried to change my nation. When I found I couldn't change the nation, I began to focus on my town. I couldn't change the town and as an older man, I tried to change my family. Now, as an old man, I realize the only thing I can change is myself, and suddenly I realize that if long ago I had changed myself, I could have made an impact on my family. My family and I could have made an impact on our town. Their impact could have changed the nation and I could indeed have changed the world." (author unknown)

Jesus tells us that the "last will be first, and the first will be last." When we look last to the reshaping of someone else's character and first to improving ourselves, we are freed from another's arrogance, negativity, and duplicity. We celebrate our gifts, realizing all good flows from the divine. Also as we champion others and take joy in their successes, our own happiness grows and grows. If you are experiencing a troubling relationship, look within and ask what is this situation asking of you. Focus on what you can change; therein lies your hope.

Get Over It

"I DON'T BELIEVE a word of it. You're seeing what you want to see. He's dead. The sooner you accept it, the sooner you can put the past behind you" Peter pleads with Thomas: "I saw him myself; you've got to believe me. Thomas lashes out, "Unless I see the nail marks in his hands and put my hand into his side, I will not believe it."

It's the following Sunday. Thomas joins the others in that same locked room. And it happens again. The Lord stands before them. "Shalom, peace be with you." The blood drains from Thomas' face. Without rancor or sarcasm, Jesus tells Thomas. "Put your finger here, see my hands." Thomas recoils. Not out of fear, really, but from a mixture of amazement and shock at the penetrating wounds. Jesus begins to open his outer garment and says, "Reach out your hand and put it into my side. Stop doubting and believe." Shamed by his unbelief, Thomas sobs. Jesus reaches out and puts a hand on his shoulder. Thomas falls to his knees and utters "My Lord and my God!"

"Doubting Thomas," delivers the greatest confession of faith recorded anywhere in the Bible. Just as Jesus embraced Thomas through his questioning, our Lord embraces us. He understands that we will question -- particularly when life falls apart -- as it will at times. He waits to show you his wounds -- not to berate you but to beckon you into his divine protection and divine intercession. Believe.

Discipleship – It Ain't Easy

WHEN JESUS SAID, "If you are going to follow me, you have to take up a cross," it was the same as saying, "Come and bring your electric chair with you. Take up the gas chamber and follow me." He did not have a beautiful gold cross in mind—the cross on a church steeple or on the front of your Bible. Jesus had in mind a place of execution. (Billy Graham)

To attract followers Jesus might have played down the pain and played up the power. Remember the scribe who pledges his loyalty and promises to accompany our Lord wherever the journey leads. Jesus might have put his arm around the man and saluted his decision: "Super! You are joining the most special team in the history of the world. This will be the best decision of your life." Instead Jesus talks about loneliness, unpredictability, and about walking away from the comforts of life. No one can accuse Jesus of sugar- coating discipleship

Following Jesus on his terms means embracing our cross. There's simply no way to follow and not feel the splinters. And are we willing to follow him NOW -- Not tomorrow, not next week, not next month. NOW! Ask our Lord, "How do you want me to follow you this day? If I am to suffer for you, give me courage to do the right thing and confidence to trust that your grace will sustain me."

New Math

A TEACHER ASKED A BOY THIS QUESTION: "Let's suppose your mother baked a pie and there were seven of you - your parents and five children. What part of the pie would you get"? "A sixth,? replied the boy. "I'm afraid you don't know your fractions,? said the teacher. 'remember, there are seven of you.? "Yes, teacher,? said the boy, "but you don't know my mother. Mother would say she didn't want any pie.' *(Bits and Pieces)*

The little boy knew the heart of his mother. Such love also filled the moments shared by Jesus and his Mother; such love bonded Cousin John with Aunt Elizabeth. It's not surprising that Mary and Elizabeth embraced so joyfully when they celebrated their pregnancies. Neither could contain their joy for the other. That initial hug of Mary and Elizabeth is a hug like no other in the history of humanity. It resonates an understanding of the awesome role of the two women – a role that proclaims the Divine's choice of the lowly as the most magnificent.

Like Mary, Christ is growing in us. No matter how insignificant our life may seem, he is forming himself through the challenges, gifts, and inexplicable sufferings of this day. If we go with eager wills, "in haste," to wherever our circumstances direct us, we can rely on Jesus to be our constant companion. This day may we have a song of gratitude in our hearts as we ask our Mother Mary for her special hug!

$108,000 Putt

AS PROFESSIONAL GOLFER RAY FLOYD was getting ready to tap in a routine 9-inch putt, he saw the ball move ever so slightly. According to the rule book, if the ball moves in this way the golfer must take a penalty stroke. Yet consider the situation. Floyd was among the leaders in a tournament offering a top prize of $108,000. To acknowledge that the ball had moved could mean he would lose his chance for big money.

Writer David Holahan describes as follows what others might have done: "The athlete ducks his head and flails wildly with his hands, as if being attacked by a killer bee; next, he steps back from the ball, rubbing his eye for a phantom speck of dust, all the while scanning his playing partners and the gallery for any sign that the ball's movement has been detected by others. If the coast is clear, he taps the ball in for his par. Ray Floyd, however, didn't do that. He assessed himself a penalty stroke and wound up with a bogey on the hole."

It's easy to be honorable when nothing is at stake. It's relatively painless to advise others to take the high road when our job and reputation are protected. But what happens when the pressure fatigues our day and night and happiness that once came so naturally has left town? Jesus urges us to watch out for the thorns of life - that which separates us from our soulful identify. Nothing, absolutely nothing, is worth the surrender of our connectivity with the Lord. The Body of Christ is with you today. His love and wisdom speak through the people in your life. Take the time to call someone who could support and guide through you difficulty.

Mechanical Rabbit

LIFE HAD CHANGED DRAMATICALLY for the sleek Greyhound. The days of the race track were gone forever. Now as the rescue dog's young owner petted him, the child asked the Greyhound if he missed the glitter and excitement of the track. "Nope," responded the dog. The boy wondered if the dog had gotten too old to race and simply couldn't keep up with his pals. "Nope," answered the dog. Perhaps the dog simply wasn't very competitive --- didn't win much money. Or maybe he was treated poorly by his owner. The Greyhound shook his head. "I won over a million dollars for my owner, and he treated me royally while I was racing." The boy finally blurted out, "Then why did you quit?" The dog stared for awhile and then answered. "I discovered that what I was chasing was not really a rabbit – just a mechanical rabbit. All that running and running, and running and running – what was I chasing? It wasn't even real." (author unknown)

Jesus warns us against the mechanical rabbit. In his parable about the weeds and the wheat, our Lord tells us that the weeds can disguise themselves as the real deal. Their effect is deadly - choking off the genuine wheat. Only a skilled farmer could distinguish wheat from weed. To avoid the weeds, to not give our time and energies to the mechanical rabbit, we need to ask ourselves, "What really matters most in my life?" Mechanical rabbits and weeds can be the seedbed of profound regret. Is something choking off your joy? Are you on a chase that is but an illusion for capturing happiness? What one thing could you do differently to free your spirit? It's all about choices. You still have time to grab your truth. Keep yourself in the "sonlight" and illusions will be revealed. Remember that an abundant life is God's personal promise to you!

The Appointment

It was a busy morning, approximately 8:30 am, when an elderly gentleman in his 80's, arrived to have stitches removed from his thumb. He stated that he was in a hurry since he had an appointment at 9:00 am The gentleman explained that he needed to go to the nursing home to eat breakfast with his wife who suffered from Alzheimer's disease. As the doctor finished dressing the man's wound, the physician asked why the man would be worried if he would be a bit late. The patient explained that his wife no longer knew who he was -- that she had not recognized him in five years. The physician was amazed. "And you still go every morning, even though she doesn't know who you are?" He smiled as he patted the doctor's hand and said. "She doesn't know me, but I still know who she is." (author unknown)

What wisdom -- what love. No matter how this man's actions were judged -- perhaps with great admiration -- perhaps with criticism for subjecting himself to unnecessary grief -- he knew a truth that transcended others' opinions. And nothing would keep him from those daily visits with his wife. Jesus urges us to stay the course. Know that some will be critical of you -- no matter how much good you do and no matter how much excellence you bring to your work. Our Lord was denounced as a glutton and a drunkard -- and his cousin, John as demonic for eating and drinking so little. There just was no pleasing that crowd. We need to strengthen our internal compass, trust its accuracy, and then follow the course. If we are honest with ourselves, "Who are we really trying to please?" Today ask the Lord to empty you of ego seeking, to fill you his Spirit. Know that He will deliver a peace, joy and confidence that will fortify you to live your day for what really matters.

Bake Bread Today

The visitor to the zoo noticed one of the keepers sobbing quietly in a corner and on inquiry was told that the elephant had died. "Fond of him, was he?" the visitor asked. "It's not that," came the reply. "He's the chap who has to dig the grave." (source unknown)

It's so easy to misjudge people's motives. But sometimes people do manipulate their actions to conceal a less than noble intention. Our Lord warns us to sidestep this trap of duplicity. "Watch out, guard against the leaven of the Pharisees and the leaven of Herod." The Pharisees were in league with Herod and his supporters to destroy Jesus. Both the Pharisees and Herod used their respective powers (their yeast) to intimidate, control, and bully their followers into obedience.

We know that yeast, or leaven, is a powerful fungus that can cause a lump of dough to rise into bread. Today don't underestimate the impact of your own "yeast." Remember the words you speak and the words you do not speak will give rise to beliefs and behaviors in your department at work and in your dining room at home. Your assignment: bake the bread and let it bring health to all.

The Ransom Note

ONCE THERE WAS A CHILD who requested a bike for Christmas. The child had written a letter to Santa asking for this gift. But no bike arrived. The child then pleaded with his parents to buy him a bike for his birthday. Again no bike arrived. Nearly at wit's end the child turned to prayer and asked God to deliver a bike the following Christmas. Again no bike. Leaving church the Sunday following Christmas, the child developed a plan. The child removed the baby Jesus doll from the Nativity scene outside the church, hid it under a coat and carried it home. At home the child carefully wrapped the baby Jesus in a blanket and hid it away in a drawer. The child then sat down to write another letter. It began "Dear Mary, if you ever want to see your son alive again… (author unknown)

Though a preposterous joke, its audacity isn't too dissimilar from the Pharisees' arrogance "who began to argue with Jesus, seeking from him a sign from heaven to test him." These men refuse to be touched by our Lord's compassion, his healing, and his forgiveness of sins. The bottom line – the Pharisees don't want to change. They must be the superior ones – even superior to God's son. Jesus refuses to give the Pharisees a platform to berate him, to toy with his miracles, or to twist and turn his motives. Jesus makes it clear "I say to you, no sign will be given to this generation."

We can learn an important lesson from our Lord's exchange with the Pharisees. Don't test God to prove his power and presence. You will inevitably miss his signs. Follow him as best you can, and the signs will be there – often in the ordinary and sometimes through a delightful surprise!

Where is God?

HOLOCAUST AUTHOR ELIE WIESEL graphically recounts the hanging of three victims, one of whom is a young boy. As the heinous act is executed, someone whispers, "Where is God? Where is He?" Wiesel painfully recalls how "we had to look him full in the face. He was still alive when I passed in front of him. His tongue was still red, his eyes were not yet glazed. Behind me, I heard the same man asking: "Where is God now?" And I heard a voice within me answer him: "Where is He? Here He is—He is hanging here on this gallows.'" (*Night*)

Only a few of our Lord's apostles escape a brutal death. Jesus even foretells Peter's execution when he repeatedly asks him, "Do you love me?" Jesus predicts, "you will stretch out your hands, and someone else will fasten a belt around you and take you where you do not wish to go." (He said this to indicate the kind of death by which he would glorify God.)

Jesus repeats his question to Peter three times. Why? The Lord gives Peter three chances to back out. While we trust the love of God will sustain us, we also know the cross will thrust its weight upon us.

The essence of suffering results in not knowing why we suffer. If we could see into the future and understand the "why," the mental anguish would subside. We hold to this prediction. If we stand for our Lord, we will receive the beatings and insults meant for him. We also hold to this promise. His faithfulness is constant. And he will have the final word

What More is There?

AN OLD SAILOR repeatedly got lost at sea, so his friends gave him a compass and urged him to use it. The next time he went out in his boat, he followed their advice and took the compass with him. But as usual he became hopelessly confused and was unable to find land. Finally he was rescued by his friends. Disgusted and impatient with him, they asked, "Why didn't you use that compass we gave you? You could have saved us a lot of trouble!" The sailor responded, "I didn't dare to! I wanted to go north, but as hard as I tried to make the needle aim in that direction, it just kept on pointing southeast." That old sailor was so certain he knew which way was north that he stubbornly tired to force his own personal persuasion on his compass. Unable to do so, he tossed it aside as worthless and failed to benefit from the guidance it offered. (author unknown)

The compass is our Lord; trying to go it alone is our insanity! Jesus tells us, "Blessed are the poor in spirit, theirs is the kingdom of God." What is "poor in spirit"? This day do you seek a peace that sustains you through life's struggles that scar the heart? Might there be a loneliness that wearies you? Perhaps a particular challenge stands before you- at work--with your family--with your self? Maybe there is a longing that evades fulfillment? Is your heart aching for another's pain? Do you feel worn down by a sense of "no control" in a matter that deeply concerns you?

We realize our spirit alone is woefully inadequate to move through the minutes of our day. In recognizing our poverty of spirit, we then can call upon his spirit to lean on, to boost our confidence, to guide us on the hills and through the valleys. When our spirit unites with the Holy Spirit, surprises, comfort, and wisdom is ours. We then experience his kingdom of unconditional love. What more is there?

The Best Compliment

THE BRILLIANT PHYSICIAN and writer Oliver Wendell Holmes, Sr., and his brother John represent two radically different views on the subject of flattery. Dr. Holmes loved to collect compliments, and when he was older he indulged his pastime by saying to someone who had just praised his work, "I am a trifle deaf, you know. Do you mind repeating that a little louder?" John, however, was unassuming and content to be in his older brother's shadow. He once said that the only compliment he ever received came when he was six. The maid was brushing his hair when she observed to his mother that little John wasn't all that cross-eyed! (source unknown)

Our Lord has a compliment for you today. He wants you to receive it and act upon it. "You are the salt of the earth." He wants the world to experience your light! We shrink back from these words. He doesn't really mean it. We can think of others who are the salt of the earth. Their light shines throughout time. But we are not in that class of people. Today we are told not to dodge the compliment. Yes, you are the recipient of Christ's robust affirmation. You may wonder how this can be especially when you're feeling less than adequate about your spirituality. It's not about you conquering the darkness alone; it's about you receiving the gift of your belovedness; it's about asking the Spirit to direct your motives so you witness to the Light of the World. It's not whether you feel deserving of the praise; it's simply about receiving this truth and trusting that his light will guide you, challenge by challenge, opportunity by opportunity.

How would you live today if you really believed that Christ saw you as his special ambassador? Confident? Mission-filled? Grateful? Remember that you're not here by chance. He has allowed you to be here at this particular time to fulfill his special purpose. Receive the compliment and bring a little more hope, perhaps a little more direction to someone close at hand.

What Am I Getting
From This Anger?

NOT TOO LONG AGO a woman was interviewed about the man who had tried to set her on fire. Wrapped in bandages and in pain, the woman was asked if she hated the person who had done this to her? She thought for a split second and responded "No". When asked why not, she answered that she did not want that person to have power over her -- to consume her thoughts. She believed that she was able to forgive him, not because it helped him, but because it freed her. She needed every ounce of energy possible to make a recovery; she would not waste one ounce more on her attacker.

There was so much out of this women's control: she could not change the damage to her body; she could not change the man – but she could choose her response to her horrific circumstance. It's difficult to be a friend to others or a friend to yourself when anger consumes your thoughts. Jesus encourages us to integrate a faith of ritual with a faith of reconciliation. "So if you are offering your gift at the altar, and there remember that your brother has something against you, leave your gift there before the altar and go; first be reconciled to your brother, and then come and offer your gift."

If you are holding onto anger, ask yourself, "What am I getting from this anger?" What's the benefit and what's the loss. Jesus tells us to pray for the person who angers us – we will be set free. Today do you need an extra boost of courage to have an honest conversation with someone?Though you can't control the outcome, you can take great satisfaction in knowing you approached this person with integrity. Let your anger be an energy that alerts you to a problem and drives your desire to bring good from a difficult situation.

More than a Bridge

ONCE UPON A TIME two brothers who lived on adjoining farms fell into conflict. It was the first serious rift in 40 years. It began with a small misunderstanding, grew into a major difference, and finally exploded into bitter exchange of words. Weeks of silence then followed. One morning there was a knock on one of the brother's door. He opened it to find a man with a carpenter's toolbox. "I'm looking for a few days work" he said. "I do have a job for you. Look across the creek at that farm. That's my neighbor, in fact, it's my younger brother. Last week there was a meadow between us and he took his bulldozer to the river levee and now there is a creek between us. Well, he may have done this to spite me, but I'll go him one better. See that pile of lumber curing by the barn? I want you to build me a fence -- an 8-foot fence -- so I won't need to see his place anymore.' The carpenter said, "I think I understand the situation. Show me the nails and the post-hole digger and I'll be able to do a job that pleases you." The carpenter worked hard measuring, sawing, and nailing. About sunset when the farmer returned, the carpenter had just finished his job. The farmer's eyes opened wide, his jaw dropped. There was no fence. It was a bridge -- a bridge stretching from one side of the creek to the other! A fine piece of work -- handrails and all -- and the neighbor, his younger brother, was coming across, his hand outstretched.

"You are quite a fellow to build this bridge after all I've said and done." The two brothers stood at each end of the bridge, and then they met in the middle, taking each other's hand. They turned to see the carpenter hoist his toolbox on his shoulder. "No, wait! Stay a few days. I've a lot of other projects for you," said the older brother. "I'd love to stay on," the carpenter said, "but, I have many more bridges to build."

Jesus breaks precedent with his Jewish ancestry. He gives a new commandment. "You have heard that it was said, `An eye for an eye and a tooth for a tooth.' But I say to you, do not resist one who is evil.

43

But if any one strikes you on the right cheek, turn to him the other also." To keep the door open when we feel like dead bolting it shut is turning the other cheek. Just maintaining civility in our exchanges can be a monumental act of integrity. To bury the ego and make that first move toward beginning again takes incredible strength of character. And like the bridge builder in the story, we can sometimes help to instigate peace. At minimum we can avoid fueling the fire. Maybe peace for each person will require a separation -- and perhaps even an ultimate separation. If bitterness, depression, or fear starts overwhelming you, ask his Spirit to shield you from self-doubt and guard you from resentment that crushes hope and happiness.

The Bookends

A MAN FROM THE BACK MOUNTAINS OF TENNESSEE found himself one day in a large city for the first time, standing outside an elevator. He watched as an old, haggard woman hobbled on, and the doors closed. A few minutes later the doors opened and a young, attractive woman marched smartly off. The father hollered to his youngest son, "Billy, go get mother." (source unknown)

Unlike the elevator story God actually uses prayer to change you. So when you pray "thy will be done," you are transformed. But, if you stopped there, you would be leaving out half the story. The Gospels talk not only about submitting to God's will but also about asking God for what you need. Prayer is both about asking and surrendering. Think of the concepts "ask and you shall receive" and "thy will be done" as bookends to prayer. Most people either focus on "ask" with little thought of surrendering to his will, or they resign themselves with "thy will be done" and seldom ask at all.

In the Scriptures, Jesus prays by asking and surrendering. In a remarkable paradox, God doesn't want either extreme -- always asking or always submitting. What he wants is a dynamic mixture of the two. Today ask God for anything. But pray for the grace of genuine surrender.

44

What's Your Intent?

WITH GREAT ENTHUSIASM A LITTLE BOY approached the sales person about a special gift he was seeking for Mother's Day. Did the sales person know if the store had a selection of cookie jars? The little boy knew how much his mom loved cookies – especially chocolate chip cookies. The child was directed to a counter that displayed a large array of cookie jars – so many different types. The youngster carefully lifted and replaced each lid. When he checked out the last one, his heart sank. "Aren't there any covers that don't make any noise?" he asked.

It is so easy to conceal from ourselves the real motivation for our behavior – particularly when we judge others. Too often we judge out of our own insecurities –judging that is rooted in a wobbly self-worth. For some reason, it is easier to jump to negative conclusions about people than it is to assume the best about them. When we do this, we sometimes reveal something about ourselves - the faults we see in others are actually a reflection of our own.

It's just easier sometimes to be critical rather than to be constructive. We may decide not to improve ourselves but instead to make others look smaller by tearing them down. On occasion we may focus on other's faults to make our own faults appear smaller; magnify another's weakness to minimize our own. Of course, revenge or jealousy is an insidious motivation for judging others.

Our Lord tells us "Judge not, that you be not judged. This day before you judge another ask this most important question: "What is my intent?" If your intent originates from love, for the higher good of others, to inspire justice, then grace paves your way. Otherwise, be wary for "the measure you give will be the measure you get."

45

The Praying Hands

BACK IN THE FIFTEENTH CENTURY, in a tiny village near Nuremberg, lived a family with eighteen children. To keep food on the table, the father worked eighteen hours a day. Two of the boys desperately wanted to attend the art academy, yet they knew their father could not support them.

Unwilling to surrender the dream, the brothers worked out a pact. They would toss a coin. The loser would go down into the nearby mines and with his earnings he would support his brother's schooling. Then when that brother who won the toss completed his studies, he would support the other brother at the academy. They tossed a coin on a Sunday morning after church. Albrecht Durer won the toss and went off to Nuremberg.

His brother Albert went down into the dangerous mines and for the next four years he financed his brother, whose work at the academy was almost an immediate sensation. Albrecht's etchings, his woodcuts, and his oils were far better than those of most of his professors. By the time he graduated, he was beginning to earn considerable fees for his commissioned works.

When the young artist returned to his village, he arranged a celebration. At the dinner, he thanked his beloved brother for the years of sacrifice. His closing words were, "And now, Albert, blessed brother of mine, now it is your turn. Now you can go to Nuremberg to pursue your dream, and I will support you." But Albert said softly, "No, brother. I cannot go to Nuremberg. It is too late for me. Look … look what four years in the mines have done to my hands! I cannot even hold a glass to return your toast, much less make delicate lines on parchment or canvas with a pen or a brush. No, brother … for me it is too late."

More than 450 years have passed. Today Albrecht Durer's hundreds of masterful art pieces hang in every great museum in the world.

Countless reproductions of his art adorn people's homes and offices. To pay homage to Albert for all that he had sacrificed, Albrecht Durer painstakingly drew his brother's abused hands with palms together and thin fingers stretched skyward. He called his powerful drawing simply "Hands." The entire world almost immediately opened their hearts to his great masterpiece and renamed his tribute of love "The Praying Hands."

This story of dreams, compassion, and love parallels many of the interactions of Jesus in the scriptures. Remember the man plagued by leprosy who beseeches Jesus to cure him. This affliction was not just a dreaded health problem; it was also a dreaded social disease. Tortured by years of suffering and disfigurement and confronted by an early death, lepers were also ostracized by Jewish law. The Jews believed that God himself had laid down the harsh conditions of a leper's lot. They were all considered persistent sinners.

The leper, like the Durer brothers, holds to a dream. Would Jesus value this man who had to cover his mouth with a hand and shout out a warning of his "unclean" condition? Would the Lord come close to him? "Moved with pity, Jesus stretched out his hand and touched him, and said to him, 'I do choose. Be made clean!'" At that moment the leper returned from death – from hopeless isolation, bankrupt self-esteem, and devastating physical pain. Today let's remember who waits to touch us – regardless of our spiritual shortcomings and physical burdens. Our Lord walks next to us with his embracing compassion. Let us show our gratitude by receiving his mercy; let us be Christ to the disguised lepers who need us to draw close.

The Disguise

IT WAS A COLD WINTER'S DAY THAT SUNDAY. The parking lot to the church was filling up quickly. Church members were whispering among themselves as they walked in the church. A man leaned up against the wall outside the church and appeared to be sleeping. He had on a long trench coat that was in shreds. A hat covered his face. His shoes, riddled with holes, were too small for his feet. People eyed the homeless man and walked into the church. A few moments later the service began. The congregation waited for the minister to take his place. When the doors to the church opened, the homeless man came walking down the aisle with his head down. People gasped and whispered. The man walked up to the pulpit where he took off his hat and coat. Everyone's heart sank. There stood our preacher. No one said a word. The preacher took his Bible and laid it on his stand. "Folks, I don't think I have to tell you what I am preaching about today. If you judge people, you have no time to love them." (author unknown)

Only one time in Scriptures does Jesus act with anger – when the marketers use his Father's house for personal gain. "And he taught, and said to them, "Is it not written, `My house shall be called a house of prayer for all the nations'? But you have made it a den of robbers." At the end of Mass the priest gives the blessing to unite sacrament with service: "The Mass has ended go in peace to love and serve the Lord." We are expected to live these words at our desk and in the family room. Our faith should move us from the pew to the poor, from the chalice to the challenged. This day pray that we have the awareness to question our intent, even behind seemingly virtuous deeds. And as Mother Teresa so powerfully realized, may we see through the poverty and realize Jesus in disguise

Where Are You Looking?

AS A LITTLE GIRL PREPARED to walk home from school, the winds whipped up, along with thunder and lightning. The girl's mother, feeling concern for her daughter, quickly got in her car and drove along the route to her child's school. As she did so, she saw her little girl walking along. At each flash of lightning, the child would stop, look up and smile.

Finally, the mother called over to her child and asked, "What are you doing?" The child answered, "Smiling. God just keeps taking pictures of me."

Who do you think smiled the most in our Lord's company? Peter probably shared a number of smiles as he proclaimed his fidelity to Jesus. Perhaps as Peter's feet eased over the water, his mouth grinned in amazement. But that moment of delight sunk into the turbulent waters. Fear overcame him. Peter could have remained in the boat like the others. But he initiated the walk to assure his friends that a ghost did not haunt the sea. His courage is significant. As long as Peter kept his eyes on Jesus and took one step at a time, he could handle the turbulence. Once Peter became focused on the strife all around him, the fisherman simply couldn't bear the pressure. Like Peter we must recognize our inability and Christ's ability. We need to remember who calms the storm and keep our eye on him. And lastly, today step out in faith and take one step at a time.

Most Important Lesson

A NURSING STUDENT shares a profound memory from her academic career. "During my second month of nursing school, our professor gave us a pop quiz. I was a conscientious student and had breezed through the questions, until I read the last one: What is the first name of the woman who cleans the school? Surely, this was some kind of joke. I had seen the cleaning woman several times. She was tall, dark-haired and in her 50s, but how would I know her name? I handed in my paper, leaving the last question blank. Just before class ended, one student asked if the last question would count toward our quiz grade. 'Absolutely,' said the professor. 'In your careers, you will meet many people. All are significant. They deserve your attention and care, even if all you do is smile and say 'hello'. I've never forgotten that lesson. I also learned her name was Dorothy." (author unknown)

The nurse's professor echoes the challenge and promise of Jesus. If you want to be great, serve. Jesus reminds us "whoever would be great among you must be your servant, and whoever would be first among you must be slave of all." To call someone by name is to affirm the person's dignity, uniqueness and significance. If we need to ask again, "What's your name?" have the humility to do so. If you meet someone new, focus on that person. Forget about impressing; take a genuine interest. Try this. Say the person's name three times in conversation. Notice the color of the person's eyes. Remembering names isn't necessarily about having a good memory. It's more about caring enough to have a trained memory. Giving of yourself in small matters will prepare you for ever greater responsibilities as the servant leader

Broken Yet Whole

A WATER BEARER IN INDIA had two large pots, each hung on the end of a pole which he carried across his neck. One of the pots was perfectly made and never leaked. The other pot had a crack in it and by the time the water bearer reached his master's house, it had leaked much of its water and was only half full. For a full two years this went on daily, with the bearer delivering only one and a half pots full of water to his master's house. Of course, the perfect pot was proud of its accomplishments. But the poor cracked pot was ashamed of its own imperfection, and miserable that it was able to accomplish only half of what it had been made to do.

After two years of what it perceived to be a bitter failure, it spoke to the water bearer one day by the stream. 'I am ashamed of myself, and I want to apologize to you.' 'Why?' asked the bearer. 'What are you ashamed of?' 'I have been able, for these past two years, to deliver only half my load because this crack in my side causes water to leak out all the way back to your master's house. Because of my flaws, you have to do all of this work, and you don't get full value from your efforts,' the pot said.

The water bearer felt sorry for the old cracked pot, and in his compassion he said, 'As we return to the master's house, I want you to notice the beautiful flowers along the path.' Indeed, as they went up the hill, the old cracked pot took notice of the sun warming the beautiful wild flowers on the side of the path, and this cheered it some. But at the end of the trail, it still felt bad because it had leaked out half its load, and so again the pot apologized to the bearer for its failure.

The bearer said to the pot, 'Did you notice that there were flowers only on your side of the path, but not on the other pot's side? That's because I have always known about your flaw, and I took advantage of it. I planted flower seeds on your side of the path, and every day while we walk back from the stream, you've watered them. For two years I have been able to pick these beautiful flowers to decorate my master's table. Without you being just the way you are, he would not have this beauty to grace his house.

We are like the cracked pot carried by the ever present Spirit. We simply must do our best to bring our Lord's highest good to others. Don't focus on your cracks. It's going to happen. Wrong decisions will be made; character flaws will dent your veneer. You will disappoint yourselves and those you love. Use the lessons from your losses to bring more compassion, communication, and comfort to those stumbling down their path. We are told that "the first will be last, and the last will be first." This is hopeful news for those with a humbled heart! Depend on our Lord. He will use all of your life experiences to nourish his kingdom.

On the Lookout

IN THE JUDEAN HILLS it was easy for a sheep to stray and become lost. When the shepherd put the sheep in the cote at night, he counted them. A sheep missing sent the shepherd on his way to track it down and bring it back to the fold. Once a sheep would realize that it was no longer with the flock, it would lie down and refuse to move, leaving the shepherd no choice but to carry it back.

Imagine the parables Jesus might have told to communicate his response to those who had distanced themselves from him -- parables that conveyed anger, abandonment or punishment to the drifter. Instead our Shepherd is not waiting for us to find our own way home to him; he is searching us out and carrying us home. No one has earned or found his or her own way into relationship with God. That relationship is wholly of grace. This day receive the Shepherd's tender love for you -- just as you are--just where you are.

The Stone in the Stream

A WISE WOMAN who was traveling in the mountains found a precious stone in a stream. The next day she met another traveler who was hungry, and the wise woman opened her bag to share her food. The hungry traveler saw the precious stone and asked the woman to give it to him. She did so without hesitation. The traveler left, rejoicing in his good fortune. He knew the stone was worth enough to give him security for a lifetime. But, a few days later, he came back to return the stone to the wise woman. "I've been thinking," he said. "I know how valuable this stone is, but I give it back in the hope that you can give me something even more precious. Give me what you have within you that enabled you to give me this stone." (author unknown)

The traveler glimpsed true happiness. He encountered a woman who championed others' good fortune. The more she shared, the more joy she experienced. The traveler realized that such happiness could never be found in things or achievements. If we find ourselves holding back our resources and gifts, we need to realize the root cause for this behavior. If our motive springs from scarcity, face this truth. Then ask our Lord to diminish your selfishness and free you from fear. Then give graciously and with an enthusiasm for the other's triumph.

As our Lord prepared to leave his friends, he prayed for them – a prayer that would give them foundational joy. "But now I am coming to you; and these things I speak in the world, that they may have my joy fulfilled in themselves." Jesus so much wants us to experience true joy—like the woman with the precious stone. Let us give our energies to cultivating a generous heart and trust that therein resides incredible happiness.

The Fate of All Great Leaders

THE SCENE SOUNDS like a James Bond movie – the crowd pressing in - taunting the hero to the brink of the precipice. But our hero isn't the Hollywood type. Though he escapes death this time, the crowd will get their wish – the brutal killing of their enemy.

Did Jesus feel terror as the crowd railroaded him toward the cliff? Did he anticipate such a violent rejection by the very people he knew the best -- friends, relatives, honored spiritual leaders. After all, he was the carpenter's son. He played games with their children, dined at their homes, made presents for their birthdays and weddings. But now Jesus was a threat. Just as Eli'jah and Eli'sha did not bring cures to the Jews but chose Gentiles, Jesus warns of a similar fate for the hometown people. He criticizes their arrogant ways; their hypocrisy that demeaned others and manipulated glory for themselves.

No doubt, Jesus could not tolerate duplicity. Consequently, he suffered the fate of all great leaders -- loneliness. Colin Powell echoes this principle: "It's inevitable; if you're honorable some people will get angry at your actions and decisions. Trying to get everyone to like you is a sign of mediocrity: you'll avoid the tough decisions, you'll avoid confronting people." Mediocre leadership is rooted in selfishness and insecurity. Pray for the grace to speak the truth. Visualize his hand upon your shoulder; his voice assuring you, "I am with you. Be confident in the Truth."

Farmer Knows Best

THERE WAS A FARMER who grew award-winning corn. Each year he entered his corn in the state fair where it won a blue ribbon. One year a newspaper reporter interviewed him and learned something interesting about how he grew it. The reporter discovered that the farmer shared his best seed corn with his neighbors. "How can you afford to share your best seed corn with your neighbors when they are entering corn in competition with yours each year?" the reporter asked. "Why, sir," said the farmer, "didn't you know? The wind picks up pollen from the ripening corn and swirls it from field to field. If my neighbors grow inferior corn, cross-pollination will steadily degrade the quality of my corn. If I am to grow good corn, I must help my neighbors grow good corn." (author unknown)

The farmer understands the connectedness of life. His corn cannot improve unless his neighbor's corn also improves. So it is in other dimensions. Those who choose to be at peace must help their neighbors to be at peace. Those who choose to live well must help others to live well, for the value of a life is measured by the lives it touches. Jesus sought to bless us with the interdependent relationship he shared with his Father. He knew that the Father's love would move us beyond a hoarding mentality – a mentality that is threatened by the accomplishments of others. He trusted that our bond with the Father would tear down any blind spots that distance us from the heartache of others.

Jesus prays fervently in the last days of his life – a bold expression of his intimate relationship with the Father and the Father with us. "The glory which thou hast given me I have given to them, that they may be one even as we are one, I in them and thou in me, that they may become perfectly one, so that the world may know that thou hast sent me and hast loved them even as thou hast loved me." If you feel like life has been a roller coaster that sometimes gets stuck at the bottom of the hill, grab tight to our Lord's words. The roller coaster will take off again Enjoy the ride!

Choose Your Wolf

AN OLD GRANDFATHER, whose grandson came to him with anger at a schoolmate who had done him an injustice, said, "Let me tell you a story. I too, at times, have felt a great hate for those that have taken so much with no sorrow for what they do. But hate wears you down, and does not hurt your enemy. It is like taking poison and wishing your enemy would die. I have struggled with these feelings many times." He continued, "It is as if there are two wolves inside me; one is good and does no harm. But the other wolf, ah! He is full of anger. The littlest thing will set him into a fit of temper. He fights everyone, all the time, for no reason. It is hard to live with these two wolves inside me, for both of them try to dominate my spirit." The boy looked intently into his Grandfather's eyes and asked, "Which one wins, Grandfather?" The Grandfather solemnly said, "The one I feed." (author unknown)

The Grandfather's wisdom beautifully parallels the words of our Lord. "Love your enemies and pray for those who persecute you, so that you may be sons of your Father who is in heaven." How do you feed your spirit to refuse the gravitational pull of a person whose behavior warrants vengeance? One thought – it is difficult to hate someone after you have prayed for them. Every time you pray for your "enemy," your hatred subsides until gradually the hatred is dissipated. Is there someone you need to pray for this day?

God Loves Him, Too?

IF YOU HAVE EVER HEARD BISHOP TUTU SPEAK, or seen him on the news, or read his book, you know that he embodies the very essence of God-given compassion and humility. Several years ago at a conference on spirituality, Tutu confessed that he needed to deepen his own spirituality to be effective in the work of reconciliation and justice in South Africa. Bishop Tutu realized that if he were to fully live the Gospel message, he must claim that God loves us. All of us. Despite giving his life to God and the church, despite a lifetime of keeping Jesus' commandments, despite hours of prayer and church-going and Bible study, Tutu had to come to terms with this truth -- God loved him no more and no less than those who oppressed and tortured his people. None of us can earn God's love and favor. We already have it! It's ours and irreversible and permanent.

Jesus reminds us that "Every one then who hears these words of mine and does them will be like a wise man who built his house upon the rock; and the rain fell, and the floods came, and the winds blew and beat upon that house, but it did not fall, because it had been founded on the rock." Live today with the guarantee that Jesus loves your least favorite person as much as you. Don't invest your energies in rooting for the other's downfall. It doesn't make sense – Godly sense. If we truly bask in God's love, it is easy to be glad that others do too.

Scars of Love

SOME YEARS AGO on a hot summer day in south Florida a little boy decided to go for a swim in the old swimming hole behind his house. He flew into the water, not realizing that as he swam toward the middle of the lake, an alligator was swimming toward the shore. His mother in the house was looking out the window saw the two as they got closer and closer together. In utter fear, she ran toward the water, yelling to her son as loudly as she could. Hearing her voice, the little boy became alarmed and made a U-turn to swim to his mother. It was too late. Just as he reached her, the alligator reached him. From the dock, the mother grabbed her little boy by the arms just as the alligator snatched his legs. That began an incredible tug-of-war between the two. The alligator was much stronger than the mother, but the mother was much too passionate to let go. A farmer happened to drive by, heard her screams, raced from his truck, took aim and shot the alligator.

Remarkably, after weeks and weeks in the hospital, the little boy survived. His legs were extremely scarred by the vicious attack of the animal. And, on his arms, were deep scratches where his mother's fingernails dug into his flesh in her effort to hang on to the son she loved. The newspaper reporter, who interviewed the boy after the trauma, asked if he would show him his scars. The boy lifted his pant legs. And then, with obvious pride, he said to the reporter, "But look at my arms. I have great scars on my arms, too. I have them because my Mom wouldn't let go." (author unknown)

We can identify with that little boy. We have scars, too. Not from an alligator, but the scars of a painful past. Some of those scars are unsightly and have caused us deep regret. But, some wounds are because God has refused to let go. He promises, "I give them eternal life, and they shall never perish, and no one shall snatch them out of my hand. My Father, who has given them to me, is greater than all, and no one is able to snatch them out of the Father's hand." In the midst of your struggle, he's been there holding on to you. This day take hope that our Lord is totally committed to your highest good and to the highest good of those you love.

Never Quit

SEVERAL YEARS AGO a 36-year-old mother was diagnosed with a terminal cancer. One doctor told her to take a lengthy vacation; another prescribed an excruciating regiment of chemotherapy and radiation – perhaps her life could be extended a bit. In a letter to her three small children, she explained: "I've chosen to try to survive for you. This has some horrible costs, including pain, loss of my good humor, and moods I won't be able to control. But I must try this, if only on the outside chance that I might live one minute longer. And that minute could be the one when you need me when no one else will do. For this I intend to struggle, tooth and nail, so help me God."

Jesus, too, "struggled, tooth and nail" – determined to be with us forever. He tells us we are his family – family ties that go deeper than that of brother and sister, mother and child. When times are confusing, challenging, and even a bit frightening, it's easy to drift away from his promise ---"you are my mother; you are my brother; you are my sister."Though we probably will drift, the promise remains true and alive. Today remind yourself of the promise and walk a bit lighter. Pass on that family love to someone close at hand but distant, or to someone distant who needs to know you are close.

Three Wishes

ONCE UPON A TIME a woman was golfing when she hit her ball into the woods. Looking for the ball, she found a frog in a trap. The frog said to her, "If you release me from this trap, I will grant you three wishes. And whatever you wish for, your husband will get 10 times more or better!" The frog was freed and the woman began her request. For her first wish she wanted to be the most beautiful woman in the world. The frog warned her, "This wish will also make your husband the most handsome man in the world-- women will flock to him." The woman replied, "That will be okay because I will be the most beautiful woman, and he will only have eyes for me". And so it was. For her second wish, she wanted to be the richest woman in the world. The frog said, "That will make your husband the richest man in the world, and he will be ten times richer than you." The woman said, "That will be okay because what is mine is his and what is his is mine." And so it happened. The frog then inquired about her third wish. The woman had grown very jealous and envied her husband, and hence she answered, "I would like a mild heart attack."

What a wicked request! Indeed jealousy deteriorates the heart. Fear drives its engine. Fear of not measuring up to the other -- in possessions, attributes, professional and family success. Enough is never enough because the yardstick changes based on the people one brushes up against that day. Gratitude is forgotten since scarcity in thought dominates. When the religious leaders listened to Jesus speak, they could not bear his wisdom. Filled with jealousy, they take "offense at him." They justify their right to discard his teaching and therein miss their sacred opportunities. Don't miss your sacred opportunities today. Avoid comparisons --monitor your self- avoid talk that denounces yourself or the other. Try to acknowledge two big blessings in your life. And if you see that frog, maybe just go back to golfing.

How Will I Be Judged?

IF YOU HAD A CHANCE to ask Jesus one question, what would it be? Try this one. "Can you tell me, Jesus, how you will judge me at the moment of my death?" I'm sure we can imagine all types of criteria that would not figure into the equation. Can you imagine Jesus scanning your dress and determining the merits of your style? Do you think he would ask, "Now tell me, before you crossed over exactly how much money did you have in your 401K?" Would he ask about your children's SAT scores or the number of times they made first honors? Doubtful. Would he be curious about the appraised value of your house? Not at all. Would he give you extra points if you had lost 10 pounds and fit into your clothes better? Not even on his radar screen. Did you ever hear him praise his apostles for such accomplishments? Of course, not.

Then what will our Lord ask us when his eyes meet ours? Really think about that. His question will no doubt be particular to your situation. The essence of the inquiry, however, will be the same for all: "Did you see me in the broken hearted and in those who broke hearts? Did you recognize me in the 'distressing disguise of the poor' – poverty of spirit and poverty of existence." Then that moment of all moments will arrive. Live your day so our Lord will say to you, "Welcome home. I'm so proud of you!"

A Victory Like No Other

AT THE SEATTLE SPECIAL OLYMPICS several years ago, nine contestants, all physically or mentally disabled, assembled at the starting line for the 100 yard dash. At the gun, they moved out, not exactly in a dash, but with a strong desire to finish the race and to win. One boy, however, stumbled on the asphalt, tumbled over a couple of times and began to cry. The other eight heard the boy, slowed down and looked back. Every one of them hurried over to help the fallen youngster. All nine linked arms and walked across the finish line together. Everyone in the stadium stood -- cheering for several minutes.

Why? These Special Olympians held the pearl of great price in their hearts. They knew what really mattered; they put aside individual glory for greater glory. To afford "the pearl of great price," we need to slow down and ask, "How are we really doing?" It's so easy to let our eyes be distracted by other treasures – the ones that satisfy for a brief time and then lose their charm. What matters most in this life is more than winning for ourselves. It's helping others win, even if it means adjusting our pace or even changing our course. It's about remembering to place ourselves wholly in God's timing and his divine protection; it's embracing our journey to find our voice and to help others find theirs.

Keep the Conversation Going

In 1883 John Roebling, a creative engineer, was inspired to build a spectacular bridge connecting New York with Long Island. Bridge building experts, however, thought this was an impossible feat. Roebling remained undaunted. After much discussion and persuasion he convinced his son, an aspiring engineer, to embrace his idea. Construction of the bridge finally began. Within only a few months on the project, a tragic accident occurred. John Roebling was killed and his son suffered serious injuries stripping him of his ability to walk, talk or even move. All he could do was simply move his finger.

One day he touched his wife's arm with that finger, indicating his desire to call the engineers. He used the same method of tapping her arm to tell the engineers what to do. For 13 years Roebling's son tapped out his instructions with his finger on his wife's arm. Today the spectacular Brooklyn Bridge stands in all its glory as a tribute to the triumph of one man's indomitable spirit, a tribute to the engineers and their team work, and a monument to the love and devotion of his wife. (author unknown)

The Scriptures present us with several women governed by such a persevering spirit. Take the Canaanite woman, who begs for her daughter's cure. Only in two places in the New Testament does Jesus praise someone for their "great faith." Curiously, both are gentiles and one is the woman from Cana. The apostles and Jesus purposely move away from the crowds for some respite. But Canaanite woman pursues Jesus. Though he appears to rebuff her requests, the distraught woman begs for a morsel of his help. Jesus fulfills her plea. "O woman, great is your faith! Let it be done for you as you wish." And her daughter was healed from that hour.Let's learn from the Canaanite woman: sincere of heart, dedicated to another, and unwavering in faith. Keep the conversation going. We know he listens!

Never Forget It

A LITTLE GIRL NAMED LIZ suffered from a rare and serious disease. Her five-year-old brother had miraculously survived the same disease and had developed the antibodies needed to combat the illness. Her only chance for recovery appeared to be a blood transfusion from her little brother. The doctor explained the situation to the boy and asked if he would be willing to give his blood to his sister. He hesitated for only a moment before taking a deep breath. "Yes, I'll do it if it will save her." As the transfusion progressed, he lay in bed next to his sister and smiled -- seeing the color return to her cheeks. Then his face grew pale and his smile faded. He looked up at the doctor and with a trembling voice asked, "Will I start to die right away?" Being young, the little boy had misunderstood the doctor; he thought he had to give his sister all of his blood to save her. (author unknown)

The unconditional love of brother for sister resonates in the Transfiguration of Christ. Our Lord knew that his closest friends would witness his suffering and crucifixion. Death would certainly appear the champion; talk of the Resurrection would appear a pitiful memory. To help his friends, Jesus took them up on Mount Tabor and gave them a glimpse of his heavenly glory. After the experience was over and they were descending the mountain together, Jesus might have cautioned Peter, James and John: "Remember, things aren't always what they seem! I know in many ways I may seem to be an ordinary man: I eat, I sleep, I laugh and I cry just like you all do. But the fact is -- I am NOT an ordinary man. You just saw that truth attested on this mountain. Never forget it!" The omnipresent divine spark pulses forward to connect with you. How incredible that our God's nature is total compassion and total magnificence! Hold to that truth and trust that your destiny is charted with profound meaning.

The Secret of a Happy Marriage

"HAVE YOU NOT READ that the one who made them at the beginning 'made them male and female,' and said, 'For this reason a man shall leave his father and mother and be joined to his wife, and the two shall become one flesh'?

A man and woman had been married for more than 60 years. They kept no secrets from each other except that the little old woman had a shoebox in the top of her closet. She had cautioned her husband never to open or ask her about it. For all of these years, he never thought about the shoebox, but one day the little old woman got very sick and the doctor said she would not recover. Eventually the wife became seriously ill. As he began to gather their documents, the little old man took down the shoebox and took it to his wife's bedside. She agreed that it was time that he should know what was in the shoebox.

When he opened it, he found two crocheted dolls and a stack of money totaling $25,000. He asked her about the contents. "When we were to be married," she said, "my grandmother told me the secret of a happy marriage was to never argue. She told me that if I ever got angry with you, I should just keep quiet and crochet a doll." The husband was so moved; he had to fight back tears. Only two precious dolls were in the shoebox. She had only been angry with him two times in all those years of living and loving. Full of gratitude, he asked, "Honey, that explains the dolls, but what about all of this money? Where did it come from?" "Oh," the little old woman said, "That's the money I made from selling the dolls." (author unknown)

No doubt, marriage has its glorious and not so glorious times. But through it all, love forgives a multitude of sins, and love celebrates the awesome gift of being the beloved of another. Today take that moment to say, "I love you." And if your spouse has passed on, know that his/her eternal soul still loves you, remembers you, and celebrates you more now than ever before!

It's Never Too Late

At 87 years of age Rose was having the time of her life. She had decided to pursue her college degree. When asked by another student what inspired her decision, Rose replied, "I always dreamed of having a college education and now I'm getting one!" Over the course of the year, Rose became a campus icon, easily making friends wherever she went... At the end of the semester the football team invited Rose to speak at their banquet. As she began to deliver her prepared speech, she dropped her three- by- five cards on the floor. Frustrated and a little embarrassed she leaned into the microphone and simply said "I'm sorry I'm so jittery. I gave up beer for Lent and this whiskey is killing me! I'll never get my speech back in order so let me just tell you what I know.

"We do not stop playing because we are old; we grow old because we stop playing. There are only three secrets to staying young, being happy and achieving success. You have to laugh and find humor every day. You've got to have a dream. When you lose your dreams, you die. We have so many people walking around who are dead and don't even know it! Have no regrets. The elderly usually don't have regrets for what we did, but rather for things we did not do. The only people who fear death are those with regrets."

At the years end Rose finished the college degree she had begun all those years ago. One week after graduation Rose died peacefully in her sleep. Over two thousand college students attended her funeral in tribute to the wonderful woman who taught by example that it's never too late to be all you can possibly be. (author unknown)

Jesus has a similar message for us. The kingdom is not based on human standards of justice and equity but on the infinite mercy of God. Perhaps there are days when you feel like the laborer who worked the 12 hour shift -- ticked at the people who received a full days pay for a measly one hour of work. But no doubt there are other days when you joined the laborers late in the day – those days where self-interest crowded out his Spirit. We are so fortunate that our God is so generous; he remembers the thief on the cross. He remembers us today – we need simply to renew our promise and try again to follow him. Give our Lord a "High Five" and move through your day with a heart of gratitude. All will be well in God's plan.

A Shepherd
Knows Commitment

A SHEEP HAS NO SENSE OF DIRECTION and no instinct for finding its way home. Lost sheep usually walk around in endless circles. When grazing they are unable to move to a new range even if they eat all the grass. If not led to green pastures, they will continue to eat the stubble of the old pasture until they starve to death. Most animals are able to smell water at a distance, but not sheep. If they wander too far from their own pasture, they cannot sense a water hole though it may be near. Sheep are almost entirely defenseless. They can't kick, scratch, bite, jump, or run. If a full-wooled sheep falls on its back, it is often unable to roll back onto its feet. In most cases it will simply give up and die unless a shepherd comes to its aid. When a sheep lies on its back for a long time, its circulation will stop. The shepherd will need to carry the 110 pound sheep for an hour or more before it is able to walk again on its own. Now that's commitment!

Take comfort in knowing that our Good Shepherd is ever vigilant for our well-being and the well-being of our families. It is contrary to our Lord's nature not to search for us. Remember he loves your children, your spouse, your mom and dad, your grandkids, your best friends, your cherished pets --- even more than you do! Be persistent in your prayers as our Good Shepherd is persistent in his search

What Kind of People Live Here?

A YIDDISH FOLK TALE tells of an old man who sat outside the walls of a great city. When travelers approached, they would ask the old man, "What kind of people live in this city?" The old man would answer, "What kind of people live in the place where you came from?" If the travelers answered, "Only bad people live in the place where we came from," the old man would reply, "Continue on; you will find only bad people here." But if the travelers answered, "Good people live in the place where we came from," then the old man would say, "Enter, for here too, you will find only good people."

It's been said that we see the world not as it is but as we are. The old man was indeed extremely wise. During Jesus' time, many doubted anyone great could originate from Nazareth. There is no mention of Nazareth in the Old Testament, the Talmud, or by the ancient Jewish historian, Josephus. In Jesus' day Nazareth was a small village -- well off the beaten track. When Philip saw Nathanael and reported that he had found the one who had been foretold by Moses and the prophets, Nathanael's response is understandable. "Can anything good come out of Nazareth?"

Christ looked into the depths of Nathanael's soul and perceived his potential -- his goodness. Christ looked, not with careless eyes, but with eyes that discovered miracle and wonder in the common and ordinary. It was Christ, who rose out of an insignificant town and made a difference to the whole world. From the ordinary came divine love. If today you doubt you own abilities -- if you look at your value with harsh eyes -- remember who gazes into your soul. See yourself as he sees you. Your greatest champion encourages you onward today!

Taxes. Tragedy. Design

A MOTHER HAD TAKEN her young toddler son to Acapulco. While the child was playing on the beach, he spotted a shiny coin. In a split second, he had put it in his mouth and began to choke. "Help my boy! Please somebody! she cried. Just then, an American came over, wrapped his arms around the child and gave a quick thrust inwards. Out popped the quarter. The mother exclaimed, "It's a miracle! Wouldn't you know God placed a doctor here so my little boy would be saved?" "Oh, I'm not a doctor, ma'am," he said. "I'm from the IRS. Getting people to cough up money is just what I do!" (author unknown)

Peter had his own run in with the IRS of his day. Since Jesus and his disciples had been away from Capernaum, they still needed to pay the tax that would support the religious activities of the temple in Jerusalem. The Pharisees and Sadducees frequently argued over this tax. The Pharisees believed that one had to pay it (in accordance with Exodus 30:13). The Sadducees, on the other hand, thought the tax was only applicable during the time of Moses. Or at most, a one time tax. So Jesus chooses to pay the fee and keep himself untangled from the politics of the day. Let the four drachmas support the upkeep of the temple. Jesus needs to focus his energies on the momentous undertaking before him – his horrific suffering and death and the Resurrection that follows. It's one thing to understand intellectually what will take place – but the living through the darkness before the light is quite another experience – even for Jesus.

Yet our Lord promises us that our life is like a piece of fine embroidery. On one side of the cloth, the threads look very random, with no sense or pattern. This is how we see life now. However, on the other side, there is design and beauty. This is the way we will see things in the future. Hold on to that hope – remember the Resurrection is the rest of the story!

Is the Water Over His Head?

IN ALASKA A LITTLE BOY went on an afternoon fishing expedition with his father. When the sight of the shore started to shrink away, the child asked, "Daddy is the water over my head." The father laughed and replied, "Way over your head, son." A few moments later came the next question, "Daddy, is it over your head, too?" This time the father heard the change in his son's voice. The father killed the boat's engine and sat down next to his boy. "Yes, son, it's quite a bit over my head, too." After a few moments, the father asked, "Son, do you want to know anything else?" The boy asked the big question, "Is the water over God's head?" The father shared that no water could ever be over God's head.

Life is full of transitions - moving, starting a new school year, getting married, becoming a parent, losing a loved one, starting a new job, being laid off. It's important to let God help you in the midst of your transitions. Don't worry that it's wrong to be going through a crisis. In fact, it's normal to undergo many different crisis situations in life. Remind yourself that God sees your destination, but you can only see one step at a time. Understand that God has a purpose for allowing you to go through each crisis; he will be with you along the way. Ask God to reveal His timing for when you might leave a situation and begin a new one.

Have courage to act according to what's best, rather than according to pressure from others. If you leave your old set of circumstances, ask God to heal your spirit so you don't enter new circumstances carrying old wounds. Acknowledge God as the ultimate source of everything you have and trust God to provide everything you need for making a transition. Don't limit the ways in which you invite God to work in your life. Be open to accepting God's creativity. Remember anything is possible with God.

The Trap

IF YOU COULD GO BACK IN TIME and approach Jesus, what would you ask Him? Perhaps like the rich, young man, you would ask our Lord the most pivotal of all questions, "Am I on the right path to be with you for eternity?" Unfortunately the wealthy youth in the Gospel grasps for immediate success and by-passes enduring happiness. In many ways the fate of African monkeys is metaphor not only for the rich, young man but also for us. African hunters have a clever way of trapping monkeys. They slice a coconut in two and cut a hole at the face of one of the halves of the shell. It will be just big enough for a monkey's hand to pass through. Then they place an orange in the other coconut half and then the two halves are fastened together. Finally, the coconut is placed on a tree with a rope.

Sooner or later, an unsuspecting monkey smells the delicious orange and discovers its location inside the coconut. Then it slips its hand through the small hole, grasps the orange, and tries to pull it through the hole. Of course, the orange won't come out; it is too big for the hole. Even when the monkey sees the hunters approaching, it does not release the orange and run away. Instead, it becomes even more frantic to take the orange with it. The poor, foolish animal is entrapped by its own greed for it cannot have both the orange and its freedom at the same time.

Sometimes we are very much like the rich, young man and the monkey. On the one hand we, too, might pray, "Save me, O God; please save me. Only do not ask me to let go of the orange." Ask yourself, "What's inside of my coconut causing me to lose my focus -- distracting me from our Lord's abundant love—diluting my choice to love others with abundant generosity? Face this question honestly. Take a small step today!

Tight Tongue; Tall Order

A WOMAN REPEATED a bit of gossip about a neighbor. Within a few days the whole community knew the story. Later, the woman responsible for spreading the rumor learned that it was completely untrue. She was very sorry and went to a wise old sage to find out what she could do to repair the damage. "Go to the marketplace," he said, "and purchase a chicken, and have it killed. Then on your way home, pluck its feathers and drop them one by one along the road." Although surprised by this advice, the woman did what she was told. The next day the wise man said, "Now, go and collect all those feathers you dropped yesterday and bring them back to me."

The woman followed the same road, but to her dismay the wind had blown all the feathers away. After searching for hours, she returned with only three in her hand. "You see," said the old sage, "it's easy to drop them, but it is impossible to get them back. So it is with gossip. It doesn't take much to spread a rumor, but once you do you can never completely undo the wrong." (author unknown)

This woman initially gains a false sense of importance by appearing superior to her neighbor. Be careful of the insidious way gossip can masquerade itself – sometimes as "concern" for others. Gossip will seem more palatable if it first hides behind this deceptive motive. "I hate to say anything about this to you, but I'm 'concerned' about so and so." In reality, the person is not sincerely concerned about solving the problem, only in talking about it -- stirring it up. Today before you pass on information about another person ask yourself, "What is my intent?" This question will stop you in your tracks or move you forward down a constructive path. These words can help us escape the duplicity of the Pharisees who "clean the outside of the cup and of the plate, but inside are full of greed and self-indulgence."

Keep Climbing

THERE ONCE WAS A BUNCH of tiny frogs who arranged a running competition. The goal was to reach the top of a very high tower. A big crowd had gathered around the tower to see the race and cheer on the contestants. The race began. No one in the crowd really believed that the tiny frogs would reach the top of the tower. Some hollered, "Oh, WAY too difficult!!" "They will NEVER make it to the top". "Not a chance that they will succeed. The tower is too high!" The tiny frogs began collapsing. One by one -- except for those who in a fresh tempo were climbing higher and higher. The crowd continued to yell, "It is too difficult!!! No one will make it!" More tiny frogs got tired and gave up. But ONE continued higher and higher and higher. At the end, everyone else had given up except for the one tiny frog. After a big effort, he was the only one who reached the top! THEN all of the other tiny frogs naturally wanted to know how this one frog managed to do it? The answer -- it turned out that the winner was deaf! (author unknown)

Jesus also ignores the critical voices – particularly that of the Pharisees. Repeatedly they chastise Jesus for his magnificent acts of love and even plot how they will bring him down. The Pharisees blind themselves with rigidity. They behave from a mind set that clings to self-worth by tearing down the noble efforts of others. Maybe you, too, have been wrongly judged. You have brought good, motivated by a sincere heart. You are shocked that others have criticized your deeds; they have attributed corrupt motives to your well-intentioned acts. Take heart. You are one with the Lord. Go forward remembering the words of Mother Teresa. "If you are kind, people may accuse you of selfish ulterior motives. Be kind anyway."

No More "I Can'ts"

A FOURTH GRADE TEACHER named Donna encouraged her students to fill out a sheet of notebook paper labeled "I Can'ts". One little girl wrote: "I can't kick the soccer ball past second base." "I can't do long division with more than three numerals." "I can't get Debbie to like me." Even the teacher participated in the exercise. "I can't get John's mother to come for a teacher conference." "I can't get my daughter to put gas in the car." "I can't get Alan to use words instead of fists." The students were then instructed to fold the papers in half and bring them to the front. They placed their "I Can't" statements into an empty shoe box. Donna added hers. Donna then marched the students out of the school to the farthest corner of the playground. There they began to dig. The box of "I Can'ts" was placed in a position at the bottom of the hole and then quickly covered with dirt.

Donna announced, "Boys and girls, please join hands and bow your heads. Friends, we gathered here today to honor the memory of 'I Can't.' While he was with us here on earth, he touched the lives of everyone, some more than others. We have provided 'I Can't' with a final resting place and a headstone that contains his epitaph. He is survived by his brothers and sisters, 'I Can', 'I Will', and 'I'm Going to Right Away'. They are not as well known as their famous relative and are certainly not as strong and powerful yet. Perhaps some day, with your help, they will make an even bigger mark on the world. May 'I Can't' rest in peace and may everyone present pick up their lives and move forward in his absence." (author unknown)

The apostles must have struggled with "I Can't." Jesus tells them "whoever does not welcome you then shake the dust off your feet as a testimony against them." What! "I can't just walk away without cursing those fools. I can't just move on without replaying over and over how mistreated I was. "I can't give up my frustration, anger, and feelings of retaliation." On the other hand some might have whispered in fear, "I can't shake the dust off my feet. I might be criticized; someone might try to pull down my reputation. The apostles might have reasoned "I can't continue to bring the good news and cure their sick -- when I'm so unappreciated.". Do you own any "I Can'ts" that hold you back? Admit it. Bury them. Let "I Can" move you forward for him.

Give What You Have: Depend on Him For the Rest

SOME OF THE MOST accomplished people have faced significant obstacles in their lives. A sampling of the list includes: * Booker T. Washington was born in slavery. * Thomas Edison was deaf. * Abraham Lincoln was born of illiterate parents. * Lord Byron had a club foot. * Robert Louis Stevenson had tuberculosis. * Alexander Pope was a hunchback. * Admiral Nelson had only one eye. * Julius Caesar was an epileptic.

But these men made history in spite of their handicaps. And there was Louis Pasteur, so near-sighted that he had a difficult time finding his way in his laboratory without glasses. There was Helen Keller, who could not hear or see, but who graduated with honors from a famous college.

Facing obstacles in your life? Take comfort from the Gospel account of the loaves and fishes. Five thousand people to feed and a mere five loaves and two fish. When Jesus asks for any remnants of food, the apostles could have scoffed at him – laughed in his face – to think something could be made from so little. Yet "all ate and were filled; and they took up twelve baskets full of broken pieces and of the fish." Be willing to place before the Lord what you do have – even if it feels so meager against the challenge facing you. Take a step in trust. Do the best with what you have and unite all your efforts with the Almighty and, like the apostles, your scarcity may turn to abundance.

The Secret to Abundance

MANY YEARS AGO THREE SOLDIERS, hungry and weary of battle, came upon a small village. The villagers, suffering a meager harvest and the many years of war, quickly hid what little they had to eat and met the three at the village square, wringing their hands and bemoaning the lack of anything to eat. The soldiers spoke quietly among themselves and the first soldier then turned to the village elders. "Your tired fields have left you nothing to share, so we will share what little we have: the secret of how to make soup from stones."

Naturally the villagers were intrigued and soon a fire was put to the town's greatest kettle as the soldiers dropped in three smooth stones. "Now this will be a fine soup," said the second soldier; "but a pinch of salt and some parsley would make it wonderful!" Up jumped a villager, crying "What luck! I've just remembered where some has been left!" And off she ran, returning with an apron full of parsley and a turnip.

As the kettle boiled on, the memory of the village improved: soon barley, carrots, beef and cream had found their way into the great pot, and a cask of wine was rolled into the square as all sat down to feast. They ate and danced and sang well into the night, refreshed by the feast and their new-found friends. In the morning the three soldiers awoke to find the entire village standing before them. At their feet lay a satchel of the village's best breads and cheese.

"You have given us the greatest of gifts: the secret of how to make soup from stones", said an elder, "and we shall never forget." The third soldier turned to the crowd, and said: "There is no secret, but this is certain: it is only by sharing that we may make a feast". And off the soldiers wandered, down the road. (author unknown)

How easy it is to feel like those villagers. I need to conceal my resources -- there may not be enough left for me. Or maybe we simply don't believe we even have much to offer....so why bother. In the Gospel there is an assumption – you are the light; you must lesson the darkness of others.

Take a moment to pray for two people who don't even know that you are beseeching the Lord for them. And here's the promise. You will be given more! "More of what, you may ask." More of what matters most -- a peaceful heart, a joyous spirit, a confidence to move with conviction.

Samurai Lesson

A ZEN STORY TELLS OF A HUGE, rough samurai who went to see a little monk to acquire the secrets of the universe. "Monk teach me about heaven and hell." The little monk looked up at the mighty warrior in silence. Then, after a moment, he said to the samurai with utter disdain, "Teach YOU about heaven and hell? I couldn't teach you about anything. You're dirty. You smell. Your blade is rusty. You're a disgrace, an embarrassment to the samurai class. Get out of my sight at once. I can't stand you!" The samurai was furious. Speechless with rage, he pulled out his sword and raised it above the monk's head, preparing to slay him. "That's hell." said the little monk quietly. The samurai was overwhelmed. He was stunned by the compassion and surrender of this little man who had offered his life to give this teaching about hell! He slowly lowered his sword and filled with gratitude, the samurai experienced a peace he could not explain. "And that's heaven," said the monk softly. (author unknown)

When we allow other's treatment of us to control our spirits, we have entered into a downward spiral. No one can make us feel a certain way unless we give that person permission. Jesus warns us about the ultimate downward plummet -- an eternity bereft of joy, peace, and ever present love. Precisely out of love, the Lord must confront us with the brutal truth of hell while ceaselessly tossing the life preserver to us. No matter how many times we drop the preserver, he will throw it our way. Today just keep your hands open; the preserver will be there.

The Kids Surprised Everyone

ONE SUMMER DAY a young boy and girl were playing in the sand. They worked very hard building an elaborate sandcastle by the water's edge. Just when they had nearly finished their project, a big wave came along and knocked it down, reducing their sandcastle to a heap of wet sand.Some of the onlookers had expected the children to burst into tears. But the kids surprised everyone. Instead, the children ran up the shore away from the water, laughing and holding hands -- and sat down to build another castle. (author unknown)

These children embody the spirit that Jesus calls us to imitate. They understand a foundational reality of life. All the things in our lives -- all the complicated structures we spend so much time and energy creating -- are built on sand. Only our relationships endure. Sooner or later, the wave will come along and knock down what we have worked so hard to build. When that happens, only the person who has somebody's hand to hold will sustain an unshakable life purpose. Pray for perspective, lighten up, and appreciate the love in your life.

Who's Your Architect?

OVER 200 YEARS AGO off the coast of Plymouth, England, a lighthouse was built to warn ships of the dangerous reefs. The architect, a man named Winstanley, was so convinced of the strength of the lighthouse that he had these words carved on the cornerstone: "Blow, O Ye Winds! Rise, O Ocean! Break Forth, Ye Elements, and Try My Work!" Less than three years later the winds did blow, the ocean did rise, and the elements did break forth to test Winstanley's work. The lighthouse along with Winstanley and his crew who were making repairs on the edifice were all swept away. Years later John Smeaton, an elderly engineer, rebuilt the lighthouse. He found a new site and dug deep into the solid rock. The new cornerstone read: "Except the Lord Build the House, They Labor in Vain that Build It." For over 90 years that lighthouse has stood every test of nature. (author unknown)

Jesus could not be clearer about the journey to greatness – let him build your house as you live as the servant helper. Are we afraid if we really live with a servant attitude we will lose competitive advantage? Perhaps we fear that our worldly value will decrease; that we will appear foolish to the ambitious -- to the high achievers. Maybe we will be called to give something up that is crucial to our identity. Where on your performance review do you receive credit for sacrificing for your co-worker, postponing your productivity -- just to bring encouragement, practical help, or a compassionate presence to someone next door, down the hall, or upstairs?

When your time to cross over arrives, Mr. or Ms. Boss will be a foggy memory. But the eye of your Lord will be upon you, and his hand will be there to clutch yours --"Welcome home. I knew I could count on you." This day be conscious of your effort to live out your greatest role in life -- to serve others.

Get in the Wheelbarrow

UPON COMPLETING a highly dangerous tightrope walk over Niagara Falls in heavy wind and rain, 'The Great Zumbrati' was met by an enthusiastic supporter. This man urged him to make a return trip --this time pushing a wheelbarrow, which the spectator had thoughtfully brought along. The Great Zumbrati was reluctant, given the terrible conditions. But the supporter pressed him, "You can do it - I know you can," he urged. "You really believe I can do it?" asked Zumbrati. "Yes - definitely - you can do it." the supporter gushed. "Okay," said Zumbrati, "Get in the wheelbarrow." (author unknown)

Getting in the wheelbarrow is precisely what Jesus did for us. He is the ultimate Good Samaritan who urges us to learn from the hero of the Gospel reading. The Samaritan's love of his neighbor proved costly. He used his own supplies to cleanse and soothe the man's wounds, his own clothing to bandage him, his own animal to carry him while the Samaritan himself walked; his own money to pay for his care, and his own reputation and credit to vouch for any further expenses the man's care would require. It's doubtful that anyone would applaud the Samaritan's sacrifice. His relatives would likely chastise his deeds. Why help someone who scorns you? But the Samaritan measured himself by his own internal standard. And for this, true greatness was his. Look for your neighbor today. Challenge yourself to extend the good will so graciously extended to us by our Good Samaritan. Don't expect "thanks" and don't look for credit. But do expect a triumphant joy within!

Why Do I feel Inferior?

A SAMURAI, a very proud warrior, came to see a Zen Master one day. The samurai was very famous, but looking at the beauty of the Master and the Grace of the moment, he suddenly felt inferior. He said to the Master, "Why am I feeling inferior? Just a moment ago everything was okay. I have faced death many times, and I have never felt any fear -- why am I now feeling frightened?" The Master said, "Wait. When everyone else has gone, I will answer." By evening the room was empty, and the samurai said, "Now, can you answer me?" The Master said, "Come outside." It was a full moon night; the moon was just rising on the horizon. And he said, "Look at these trees. This tree is high in the sky and this small one beside it. They both have existed beside my window for years, and there has never been any problem. The smaller tree has never said to the big tree, 'Why do I feel inferior before you?' This tree is small, and that tree is big -- why have I never heard a whisper of it?" The samurai said, "Because they can't compare." The Master replied, "Then you need not ask me. You know the answer."

If we accept that God totally loves each of us, we know that He never compares us. No one is more special to God because of their abilities. In the divine plan there is a reason you have been blessed with certain abilities and a divine reason you have not be given certain attributes. This day let us be freed from fears that strip our self-confidence when we negatively compare ourselves or those we love to other people. Jesus tells us to not be afraid – that even the sparrows are not forgotten in God's sight. And certainly we are more valuable than the birds of the air.

Head into the Storm

THERE IS AN OLD STORY out of the American West about how cattle act in winter storms. Sometimes the storms took a heavy toll on the animals. The storms would start with freezing rains. Temperatures would plummet below zero. Then, bitterly cold winds would begin to pile up huge snowdrifts. Most cattle turned their backs to the icy blasts and they would begin to move downwind until they came up against the inevitable barbed wire fence. In the big storms, they would pile up against the fence and die by the score. But one breed always survived. Herefords would instinctively head into the wind. They would stand shoulder to shoulder heads down, facing the blasts. As one cowboy once put it, "You most always found the Herefords alive and well. I guess that's the greatest lesson I ever learned on the prairies - just face life's storms."

Think about how Jesus faced life's storms. Unlike those cattle that turned their backs to the icy blasts, Jesus took on the hypocrisy of the Pharisees. He refused to give them a pass -- to look the other way. Their deceptions and manipulations sucked the life out of good people who wanted to love God. Maybe today you need to head into the storm? Speak up -- be willing to risk as you trust His promise. "Do not be afraid; you are of more value than many sparrows."

Tough Words

AN AMERICAN HERO, Scott Carpenter is one of our seven first astronauts. He had a passion for dedicating his life to the mission of going to the moon. Scott once remarked, "This project of being an astronaut and going to the moon gives me the possibility of using all of my capabilities and all of my interests and gifts at once. This is something that I would be willing to give my life for. I think a person is fortunate to have something that you care that much about that you would give your life for. There are risks involved, that's for sure."

Scott Carpenter loved his family completely, yet he was willing to give his life for a mission that embraced his very soul. Belonging to Jesus becomes the determining factor regarding all our values, our decisions and all our relationships. According to Jesus, when he calls someone to follow him, nothing on earth must come between him and the one he has called. Jesus asks his followers, "Do you think that I have come to bring peace to the earth? No, I tell you, but rather division!"

These are really tough words. Jesus scorns keeping the peace if it means turning our back on him. Our Lord reminds us that our life center must be him -- not our families, not our friends, not our causes. Do you need to speak the truth to a loved one today, then ask for the courage to express yourself; ask for the grace to keep your ego in check and the fortitude to bear the rejection that might follow.

Our Best for His Best

IN EARLY DECEMBER A DOCTOR visited a local grade school to encourage the children to donate toys for his medical clinic in Africa. The doctor suggested that maybe the children would like to give some of their old toys as presents. He would then talk to African children about God's greatest gift – Jesus. The children liked the idea. A week later the doctor returned to collect the gifts. He was shocked by what happened. One by one the children filed by and gave the doctor a doll or toy. But not the old toys. Oh, no. The children all gave their new presents. "Why?" the doctor wanted to know. A little girl spoke up: "Doctor, think what Jesus did for us. He gave us his best; can we do anything less?" (unknown)

The girl had it right. How can we give our best for our Lord? Start by appreciating your gifts – refrain from comparing yourself to others – step out of your comfort zone – ask for his Spirit to infuse your motivation. But it's not enough simply to cultivate your gifts. You are also called to inspire others to find their voice. Jesus clearly tells us, "From everyone to whom much has been given, much will be required; and from the one to whom much has been entrusted, even more will be demanded."

If you find new opportunities awaiting you; if you face a challenge that will tap deep into your character and into your abilities – know our Lord needs you to be his source of courage, of hope, even of change. Just do your best for his best --- and then let go of the nonsense that tries to drag you down. He has put his trust in you. What an honor!

Celebrate the Ultimate Moment

HOW DO YOU PREPARE for your moment of death? In many ways all of life is a dress rehearsal for that final goodbye. Life is a series of letting go until our last breath signals our final farewell. Jesus cautions us to be ready for the master who returns "during the middle of the night, or near dawn." An Indian Proverb reminds us of the fragility of life: "When the sun goes down at sunset remember it will take a part of your life with it." How do we seize the moment so our collective moments celebrate the ultimate moment? Few of us live days measured by extraordinary decisions, heroic behavior or revolutionary thinking. And that's fine. We still need to seize the 60 seconds of each minute so His unconditional love finds life in our work, our parenting, our leisure. What is that priceless gift that you can give away this day before the night surrenders to the dawn?

The Miser's Demand

THERE WAS A MAN who worked all of his life, saved all of his money, and lived as a miser. Just before he died, he said to his wife, "When I die, I want you to take all my money and put it in the casket with me. I want to take my money to the afterlife with me." At the man's funeral, his wife had the opportunity to fulfill her husband's request. When the ceremony concluded, the undertakers were preparing to close the casket.

The wife said, "Wait just a minute!" She came over with the box and put it in the casket. Then the undertakers locked the casket down and rolled it away. A close friend of the woman, aware of her husband's request, whispered to her friend, "I know you weren't fool enough to put all that money in there with your husband." The loyal wife replied, "Listen, I'm a Christian. I can't go back on my word. I promised him that I was going to put that money in that casket with him." Her friend responded, "You mean to tell me you put that money in the casket with him?" The wife answered, "I sure did. I got it all together, put it into my account and wrote him a check. If he can cash it, he can spend it." (unknown)

The woman's husband is an exaggeration of us -- on any given day we lose ourselves to empty promises that give us the illusion of security and importance. Today ask yourself what is enough, what is too little. We need to continue scrutinizing the role of possessions in our lives. The stronger our relationship with God becomes, the more willing we will be to listen to the voice that tells us when enough is enough. Perhaps it's time to simplify your life -- maybe "things" are crowding out your time for "things" that really matter. Enjoy your kids. Have fun with your spouse. Make a phone call, send a card, visit someone -- let your heart connect with your treasures.

Remember to RSVP

"IF YOU MEDITATE ON THE WORD GUIDANCE, you notice "dance" at the end of the word. Doing God's will is a lot like dancing. When two people try to lead, nothing feels right. The movement doesn't flow with the music, and everything is quite uncomfortable and jerky. When one person realizes that, and lets the other lead, both bodies begin to flow with the music. One gives gentle cues, perhaps with a nudge to the back or by pressing lightly in one direction or another. It's as if two become one body, moving beautifully. The dance takes surrender, willingness, and attentiveness from one person and gentle guidance and skill from the other. In meditating further on the word Guidance, you realize that "G" represents God, followed by "u" and "i". -- "God, "u" and "i" dance." God, you, and I dance. Trust that God will guide you if you but let him lead." (author unknown)

It's time to kick up your heels. Like the people in Scriptures, you have been invited to a magnificent wedding feast. But be careful. Don't delay your RSVP; don't invent excuses like the men in the gospel. "But they all alike began to make excuses. The first said to him, 'I have bought a piece of land, and I must go out and see it; please accept my regrets.'" You have a chance of a life time…an opportunity to say "yes" to the most important invitation ever sent in the history of the world.

If you are struggling with a tough decision, with illness, with conflict at work or home – if you feel off balance in the dance of life – accept where you are at this moment. Extend your hand to the master dancer. Even if you stumble step by step, he's leading – just do your best and put your trust in him. And don't forget to give yourself a pat on the back. He's happy to be your partner!

The Wisdom of the Horses

JUST UP THE ROAD live two horses, the male horse blind from an unfortunate accident. If nearby and listening, you will hear the sound of a bell. Looking around for the source of the sound, you will see that it comes from the smaller horse in the field. Attached to her halter is a small bell that lets her blind friend know where she grazes and moves throughout the field. As you stand and watch these two friends, you'll see how she is always checking on him; he will listen for her bell and then slowly walk to where she is -- trusting that she will not lead him astray. When the mare returns to the barn's shelter each evening, she stops occasionally and looks back, making sure her friend isn't too far behind to hear the bell. As the seasons change and the years accumulate, the mare may someday need a friend to protect her from the dominant, younger horses. These magnificent animals tell our story. Sometimes we are the blind horse being guided by the little ringing bell; other times we are the guide horse, helping others see. (author unknown)

Jesus reminds us of his expectation: "But when you give a banquet, invite the poor, the crippled, the lame, and the blind." Our Lord asks us to extend our hand with humility and respect -- to serve not the leftovers -- but our finest for his beloved. It is simply a matter of time when we, too, will face difficulty. We will need guidance, encouragement, a hand up -- all in a spirit that celebrates our dignity. Who needs you to ring your bell this day? Someone does. Listen. The God of all creation will direct your path.

The Drawing

A FIRST GRADE TEACHER at Thanksgiving asked her class to draw a picture of something they were thankful for. She thought of how little these children from poor neighborhoods actually had in their lives. But she knew that most of them would draw pictures of turkeys or tables with food. The teacher was taken aback with Douglas' picture--a simple, childishly drawn hand. But whose hand?

The class was captivated by the abstract image. "I think it must be the hand of God that brings us food," said one child. "A farmer," said another, "because he grows the turkeys." After the children had returned to a class assignment, the teacher bent over Douglas' desk and asked whose hand it was. "It's your hand, Teacher," he mumbled. She recalled that frequently at recess she had taken Douglas, a scrubby forlorn child, by the hand. She often did that with the children. But it meant so much to Douglas. (author unknown)

The young boy's expression of gratitude reminds us of the healed leper who turns back to thank Jesus. Of the ten, he is the only one whose soul as well as his body is healed: "Get up and go on your way; your faith has made you well." The practice of gratefulness is a spiritual practice that transforms a person. An attitude of gratitude delivers immediate results to us. When we chose to experience our day focused on gratitude, we suddenly become alert to the countless blessings in that day. God's unconditional love becomes an experience, not just a theological thought.

Here's an idea. Get a notebook, any size. At the end of the day, write the date down, and then "Gifts:" Simply jot down anything that felt like a blessing to you. Try this for one week -- you'll notice a joy and balance that sustains you through your daily challenges.

Let Go of the Branch

A MAN NAMED JACK was walking along a steep cliff one day when he accidentally got too close to the edge and fell. Fortunately he grasped a branch that kept him from plummeting more than a thousand feet. Jack began yelling for help, hoping that someone passing by would hear him and lower a rope or something. He yelled for a long time, but no one heard him. Ready to give up, he at last heard a voice from above.

"I can see you, Jack. Are you all right?"

"Yes, but who are you, and where are you?

"I am the Lord, Jack. I'm everywhere."

"God, please help me! I promise if, you'll get me down from here, I'll serve you for the rest of my life."

"Now, here's what I want you to do, Jack. Listen carefully."

"I'll do anything, Lord. Just tell me what to do."

"Okay. Let go of the branch."

"What?"

"I said, let go of the branch." Just trust me. Let go."

There was a long silence.

Finally Jack yelled, "HELP! HELP! IS ANYONE ELSE UP THERE?" (author unknown)

Ever feel like Jack? We want faith until that faith demands a leap out of our comfort zone. Could more faith mean following more closely the footsteps of Jesus – which led him to the ridicule and suffering and death on the cross? Do we really want more faith? We may want more of the faith that will help us out – a faith that might heal ourselves or a loved one, a faith that gives us the assurance of eternal life. But do we really want a faith that will make us more Christ-like? What is one way you could be more like our Lord? Something that really challenges you. Are you ready to ask in faith? He's listening

An Unlikely Pick

WITH A BIG SMILE, a little boy approached a farmer to buy one of his puppies. But the farmer discouraged the boy. "These puppies come from fine parents and cost a good deal." The boy dropped his head for a moment, then looked back at the farmer and said, "I've got thirty-nine cents. Is that enough to take a look?" The farmer responded by whistling for the dogs.

Out from the doghouse peeked a pup noticeably smaller than the others. Down the ramp it slid and began hobbling in an attempt to catch up with the others. The little boy cried out, "I want that one," pointing to the runt. The farmer knelt down and said, "Son, you don't want that puppy. He will never be able to run and play with you the way you would like." The boy reached down and slowly pulled up one leg of his trousers -- revealing a steel brace. Looking up at the farmer, he said, "You see, sir, I don't run too well myself, and he will need someone who understands." (unknown)

Our faith reminds us of a promise - that we have someone who understands - someone who will be our voice just like the little boy. When Jesus enters Capernaum, a centurion comes to him, and begs, "Lord, my servant is lying at home paralyzed, in terrible distress." And Jesus answers, 'I will come and cure him.' How amazing that the great Roman centurion - the leader of a 100 soldiers -would bother with a slave. Typically when a slave could no longer work, he was simply sent out to die. A man of great compassion and great faith, the centurion was compelled to call upon Jesus for a miracle.

When we are concerned about healing or any other crisis in our life, remember that Jesus has authority over that problem. Take comfort this day. Lord, I am not sure how you will deal with this situation, but I know you have the power to deal with it in whatever way you choose. You will work for my highest good and the highest good of my beloved family and friends. I may not understand your ways today, but I will trust in your infinite love.

Trust Our Lord's Word; Not Your Circumstance

AFTER PHYSICIST RICHARD FEYNMAN won a Nobel Prize for his work, he visited his old high school and decided to look up his records. He was surprised to discover that his grades were not as good as he remembered and his IQ was 124 -- not much above average. Winning the Nobel Prize was one thing, but to win it with an IQ of only 124 amazed Dr. Feynman. Most of us assume that the winners of Nobel prizes have exceptionally high IQs. Feynman confided that he always assumed his IQ was exceptional. If Feynman had known he was really just a bit above average in the IQ department, would he have launched his research experiments that won him the greatest recognition in the scientific community? Perhaps not.

Some times we fall short of our potential because we give our power away to those who don't recognize our gifts or to the limitations we place upon ourselves. Look at the incredible happening to a couple of many years' old -- Zachariah and Elizabeth -- decades beyond child bearing years. The angel spoke, "Do not be afraid, Zachariah, for your prayer has been heard. Your wife Elizabeth will bear you a son, and you will name him John. You will have joy and gladness, and many will rejoice at his birth, for he will be great in the sight of the Lord."

Zechariah and Elizabeth thought God had forgotten them or maybe turned away from them. The truth is that God was preparing them. His delay was purposeful. Our Lord wanted everyone to know that this was no ordinary child. God knew that each day in John's young life his parents would tell him about God's greatness and God's calling for his life. And no one who would love a child more than Zechariah and Elizabeth.

God has a purpose for the delays in our life. When times are discouraging, it's easy to think that God has forgotten us. It's tempting to look at others who seem to have everything going their way and feel that there must be something wrong with us. He may be using this hard time to teach us a valuable truth or skills that will help us in a future endeavor. Of course, it's possible that we may not understand God's purpose until we get to Heaven. This one thing is sure: God does not abandon his children. The best way to handle discouraging times is to live faithfully and trust fully like Zechariah and Elizabeth. Their circumstances were difficult but their trust remained true. They determined that they would trust the character of God rather than the circumstances of life. .When we live this principal, possibilities open up, limitations don't overshadow us, and we, too, have a wonderful future before us!

The Video Tells All

A MOTHER WAS PREPARING pancakes for her sons, Kevin 5, and Ryan 3. The boys began to argue over who would get the first pancake. Their mother saw the opportunity for a moral lesson. "If Jesus were sitting here, He would say, 'Let my brother have the first pancake, I can wait.' Kevin turned to his younger brother and said, "Ryan, you be Jesus!" (author unknown)

Kevin got it right. Jesus calls us to sacrifice. Yet many people who knew Jesus were confused by his identity. Some thought he was John the Baptist; others a prophet, or a divine leader who would restore the Jewish kingdom.

When Jesus quizzes Peter, "Who do you say that I am?" Peter triumphs. "You are the Messiah." Here's the challenge for us. Suppose your day were videotaped - unknown to you. And the video were played back before an audience of familiar and unknown people. The attendees were then given a sheet of paper with one question. "Based on the action and thoughts of the person, who is Jesus to this individual?"

How do you want your video to look today?

The Gift of Life;
The Gift of Sacrifice

EVERY YEAR IN ALASKA, a 1000-mile dogsled race, run for prize money and prestige, commemorates an original "race" run to save lives. Back in January of 1926, six-year-old Richard Stanley showed symptoms of diphtheria, signaling the possibility of an outbreak in the small town of Nome. When the boy passed away a day later, Dr. Curtis Welch began immunizing the people with an experimental but effective anti-diphtheria serum. But it wasn't long before Dr. Welch's supply ran out, and the nearest serum was in Nenana, Alaska—1000 miles of frozen wilderness away.

Amazingly, a group of trappers and prospectors volunteered to cover the distance with their dog teams! Operating in relays from trading post to trapping station and beyond, one sled started out from Nome while another, carrying the serum, started from Nenana. Pained by frostbite, fatigue, and exhaustion, the teamsters mushed on relentlessly. After 144 hours in minus 50-degree winds, the serum was delivered to Nome. Only one other life was lost to the potential epidemic. Their sacrifice had given an entire town the gift of life. (author unknown)

The sacrifice of Mary and Joseph gave all of humanity the gift of life. Can you imagine how Mary and Joseph must have moved through those first days with their astounding secret? On one hand, joyous gratitude and enthusiasm must have pulsated through their spirits. Yet, perhaps the thought crossed Joseph's mind, "Lord, maybe you could have arranged your timing a little better. Couldn't you have waited until Mary and I were just about to finalize our engagement? Couldn't you have spared us the gossip, the judgments, the cruel words? Just let us enjoy our moment without that gray cloud in the background."

It seems the gift of life demands the gift of sacrifice. We look to Mary and Joseph as our role models -- how to care for our loved ones -- with hope, patience, and often times with our share of painful moments. All of this makes sense since our God is right in our midst -- living for us. Like Mary and Joseph we embrace the greatest of all promises: "Look, the virgin shall conceive and bear a son, and they shall name him Emmanuel," which means, "God is with us."

The End of Time --
What to Do?

ON A BRIGHT DAY in May over two hundred years ago, the Connecticut House of Representatives had gathered. The delegates discussed and argued by natural light. But then something happened that nobody expected. Right in the middle of a debate, an eclipse of the sun brought total darkness. Panic took over. Some wanted to adjourn; others wanted to prepare for the coming of the Lord. But the speaker of the House had a different idea.

A Christian believer, he rose to the occasion with good logic and good faith. "We are all upset by the darkness, and some of us are afraid. But the Day of the Lord is either approaching or it is not. If it is not, there is no cause for adjournment. And if the Lord is returning, I, for one, choose to be found doing my duty. I therefore ask that candles be brought forth." (author unknown)

Everyone, including the men who expected the return of Jesus, went back to their desks and resumed their debate. Perhaps the best way to prepare for the Lord's coming is simply to do the next right thing. "To see him more clearly, love him more dearly, follow him more nearly --day by day." Think of one thing today that will demand a little more kindness, listening, sacrifice or openness. Give it your best and let his light shine through you!

The Experiment

SOME YEARS AGO, DR. KARL MENNINGER, noted doctor and psychologist, sought the cause of many of his patients' ills. One day he gathered his clinical staff and explained a plan for developing an atmosphere of creative love. All patients were to receive large quantities of love; no unloving attitudes were to be displayed in the presence of the patients. The nurses and doctors were to go about their work in and out of the various rooms with a loving attitude. At the end of six months, the patients' stay in the institution was reduced by 50%.

The power of love—affirming, healing, hopefilled. Menninger's staff dispelled the darkness and filled the patient's void with meaning and worth. Such love connects with that moment when light overcame darkness, when the divine embraced the human, when hope conquered despair. And "all who received him, who believed in his name, he gave power to become children of God, who were born, not of blood or of the will of the flesh or of the will of man, but of God. And the Word became flesh and lived among us, and we have seen his glory, the glory as of a father's only son, full of grace and truth". "And the Word became flesh and dwelt among us"

God has gone to the greatest extent to draw us back into his embrace. God the Son completely identified with us in our "fleshiness"—our weakness and frailty—by uniting himself permanently with humanity through the incarnation. God has drawn as close as possible in Christ. In doing this, God has completely identified with the human situation. This day remember who champions you; who lights your way through the shadows of doubts; who calls you to uplift the heavy of heart.

Why?

ON FEBRUARY 15, 1947, Glenn Chambers boarded a plane bound for Quito, Ecuador to begin his ministry in missionary broadcasting. In a horrible moment, the plane carrying Chambers crashed into a mountain peak and spiraled downward. Before leaving the Miami airport, Chambers wanted to write his mother a letter. All he could find for stationery was a page of advertising on which was written the single word "WHY?" Around that word he hastily scribbled a final note. After Chambers' mother learned of her son's death, his letter arrived. She opened the envelope, took out the paper, and unfolded it. Staring her in the face was the questions "WHY?"

We move from the starlit manger to the slaughter of the children. We move from the joyous voices of the angels to Mary and Joseph's flight from Bethlehem - uncertain when they would return to their peaceful life in Nazareth. Their world was dented by interruption and confusion -- pained by separation from families and friends, from all they cherished in Nazareth. The Holy Family was called to live in a strange land as refugees, alien immigrants. Our Lord was born as an outcast, a homeless person, a refugee, a victim of the powers that be. This is our Savior, who was born into the midst of terror and enters into the terror of our world every day.

No doubt, the mothers of the massacred children cried out the reverberating word, "Why?" Mary also must have wondered "Why?" as she hurried her new born into a land where she and Joseph mattered to no one. But they moved in trust - a trust uplifted by love of family -- that never abandons, never lets the circumstances become more powerful than belief in each other, and in the abiding presence of the Lord. God is with us - not in some abstract and perfect place - God is with us here and now, wherever we are on the journey.

What's Your Answer?

A YOUNG MAN was walking down the sidewalk one day when he encountered a rabbi who had taught him years before. By now the rabbi was a very old man, but they were still able to recognize each other. The rabbi asked the young man, "What have you done with your life?" His former student answered, "I have a lovely wife, two beautiful children, and an excellent job."

When the rabbi repeated the question, the younger man assumed his old teacher had grown deaf and loudly repeated his answer. Then the rabbi said, "I heard you the first time. I asked you again because you did not answer my question. You told me what God had done with your life. Now tell me what you have done." (author unknown)

How would we answer that question? Let's learn from the poor widow in Luke's gospel. Jesus marvels at her and asks his disciples to open their souls to her example: 'Truly I tell you, this poor widow has put in more than all of them; for all of them have contributed out of their abundance, but she out of her poverty has put in all she had to live on." We have no reason to believe this woman even realized that our Lord had singled her out. We have every reason to believe she had left as quietly as she came – careful not to disturb the important men and Temple leaders around her.

We are asked to serve not from our leftovers but from the main course. What does this mean for us? Maybe it's being more generous with our material possessions - maybe with our time for family, friends, and strangers, maybe with our praise, thanksgiving, and pleas to our Lord, maybe taking that hour on Sunday to dedicate ourselves at Mass. Before you close your eyes tonight, hear the rabbi's question. Let's be able to answer so we won't hear his question twice!

You Want Me To Do What?

A NOVICE MOUNTAIN CLIMBER, desperate to conquer the Rockies, initiated his climb. As he was climbing a ridge at about 100 meters from the top, he slipped and fell. Falling rapidly he could only see blotches of darkness that passed. But then he felt a jolt. Like any good mountain climber, he had staked himself with a long rope tied to his waist.

In those moments of stillness, he shouted: "HELP ME GOD. HELP ME!" Suddenly he heard a deep voice from heaven. "What do you want me to do?"

"SAVE ME."

"Do you REALLY think that I can save you?"

"OF COURSE, MY GOD."

"Then cut the rope that is holding you up."

There was another moment of silence and stillness. The man just held tighter to the rope. The next day the rescue team found a frozen mountain climber hanging strongly to a rope. -- TWO FEET OFF THE GROUND. (author unknown)

The mountain climber confronts the essential question: "Do we trust that our Lord is there for us?" In Matthew's Gospel, two blind men face this same challenge. As Jesus went on from there, two blind men followed him, crying loudly, "Have mercy on us, Son of David!" When he entered the house, the blind men came to him; and Jesus said to them, "Do you believe that I am able to do this?"

Will we throw ourselves at his mercy, release our grip and open ourselves to his all-knowing generosity? Sometimes it feels that blindness still shrouds our next step; maybe no one will be there to catch our fall. Such doubt is natural. But the refusal to release our grip closes us off to his divine surprises. This day let us beseech our Lord to remove all doubt that paralyzes us. May we receive his all protecting Spirit so we, too, hear "According to your faith let it be done to you."

More than a Spider's Web

DURING WORLD WAR II, a US marine was separated from his unit on a Pacific island. Alone in the jungle, he could hear enemy soldiers coming in his direction. Quickly he crawled inside one of the caves. Once the enemy soldiers moved up the ridge, they would quickly search all the caves, and the man would be killed.

He prayed, "Lord, if it be your will, please protect me. Whatever your will though, I love you and trust you. "After praying, he lay quietly listening to the enemy begin to draw close. He thought, "Well, I guess the Lord isn't going to help me out of this one." Then he saw a spider begin to layer strand after strand of web across the opening of the cave. "Hah, he thought." What I need is a brick wall and what the Lord has sent me is a spider web.

As the enemy drew closer, he watched from the darkness of his hideout. He could see them searching one cave after another. To his amazement, the man watched the soldiers move on after glancing in the direction of his cave. Suddenly he realized that the spider web over the entrance caused his cave to look as if no one had entered it for quite a while. "Lord, forgive me," prayed the young man. "I had forgotten that in you a spider's web is stronger than a brick wall." (author unknown)

Such providential love is experienced in the genealogy of Jesus. When Matthew looks back over the history of God's people, he chronicles fourteen generations between Abraham, David, Exile, and our Lord. When one looks back on Old Testament history through the lens of Jesus, one sees that God's hand was steady and sure. The Sovereign God is in complete control of history, assuring that His purposes and promises will be fulfilled.

We all face times of great trouble. When we do, it is so easy to forget what God can work in our lives, sometimes in the most surprising ways. Our Lord never breaks his promise to lead us with lasting purpose. Remember with God, a mere spider's web can become a brick wall of protection.

Pearly Gates

A MAN DIES and goes to heaven. Of course, St. Peter meets him at the pearly gates. St. Peter says, "Here's how it works. You need 100 points to make it into heaven. You tell me all the good things you've done, and I give you a certain number of points for each item, depending on how good it was. When you reach 100 points, you get in."

"Okay," the man says, "I was married to the same woman for 50 years and never cheated on her, even in my heart."

"That's wonderful," says St. Peter, "that's worth three points!"

"Three points?" he says. "Well, I attended church all my life and supported its ministry with my tithe and service."

"Terrific!" says St. Peter, "that's certainly worth a point."

"One point? Golly. How about this: I started a soup kitchen in my city and worked in a shelter for homeless veterans."

"Fantastic, that's good for two more points," he says.

"TWO POINTS!!" the man cries, "At this rate the only way I get into heaven is by the grace of God!"

"Come on in!" (author unknown)

Looking to receive a heavy dosage of the grace of God – simply listen to the Lord's promise: "Those who eat my flesh and drink my blood have eternal life, and I will raise them up on the last day; for my flesh is true food and my blood is true drink. Those who eat my flesh and drink my blood abide in me, and I in them." The next time you receive the Eucharist pause in awe – the Lord's guarantee is mind boggling.

Case Dismissed

WHEN A MAN IN AUSTRALIA was arrested for stealing a sheep, he claimed the animal belonged to him. When the case went to trial, the judge was puzzled, not knowing how to decide the matter. At last he asked that the sheep be brought into the courtroom. He then ordered the plaintiff to step outside and call the animal. The sheep made no response except to raise its head and look frightened. The judge then instructed the defendant to go to the courtyard and call the sheep. When the accused man began to make his distinctive call, the sheep bounded toward the door. It was obvious that he recognized the familiar voice of his master. "His sheep knows him," said the judge. "Case dismissed!" (author unknown)

Jesus, the good shepherd, knows you by name. He tells us that when the wolves approach "the hired hand runs away because a hired hand does not care for the sheep. I am the good shepherd. I know my own and my own know me, just as the Father knows me and I know the Father. And I lay down my life for the sheep." How does that make you feel? Remember this in tough times – times of loneliness and lost direction. At times all of us will feel the peering eyes of the wolf upon us. At all times the protective eyes of the Lord will keep watch over us. Maybe those eyes are disguised as a friend, a parent, a spouse, a child. Don't give the wolf too much power – stare back at the Lord, ask to hear his voice – and let him lead you to greener pastures.

The Common Preacher, Not so Common

A FAMOUS SHAKESPEARIAN ACTOR with his ascot and cigarette holder and tiny mustache was once the guest of honor at a party where several people asked him to recite favorite excerpts from various literary works. An old dried-up preacher wearing an ill-fitting polyester suit also happened to be there. The old preacher asked the actor if he would recite his favorite passage of Scripture, the twenty-third Psalm. The actor agreed on the condition that the preacher would also recite it. The actor's recitation was beautifully intoned with great dramatic emphasis for which he received lengthy applause. He turned to the preacher and said, "Now, please, you say it."

The preacher's voice was rough and broken from many years of preaching, and his diction was anything but polished. But when he finished there wasn't a dry eye in the room. The famous actor, with tears in his own eyes said emphatically, "I know the psalm, but he knows the Shepherd." (author unknown)

Our Lord guarantees us that "I give them eternal life, and they will never perish. No one will snatch them out of my hand." Kindness, forgiveness, generosity, love, and faith are the eternal things that go on forever – that change people's lives long after we are gone. This change is one person to another, and then another, and so on, and so on. Listen to the shepherd today. His voice carries a promise and a request. "I want to give you abundant life, and I need you to be my voice to the deserving and undeserving."

Keep Your Fork

THERE WAS A WOMAN who had been diagnosed with a terminal illness and had been given three months to live. So as she was getting her things "in order," she contacted her pastor and had him come to her house to discuss certain aspects of her final wishes.

She told him which songs she wanted sung at the service, what scriptures she would like read, and what outfit she wanted to be buried in. The woman also requested to be buried with her favorite Bible. Everything was in order and the pastor was preparing to leave when the woman suddenly remembered something very important to her. "There's one more thing," she excitedly. "What's that?" came the pastor's reply. "This is very important," the woman continued. "I want to be buried with a fork in my right hand." The pastor stood looking at the woman, not knowing quite what to say. "That surprises you, doesn't it?" the woman asked. "Well, to be honest, I'm puzzled by the request," said the pastor.

The woman explained. "In all my years of attending church socials and potluck dinners I always remember that when the dishes were cleared, someone would inevitably lean over and say, 'Keep your fork.' It was my favorite part because I knew that something better was coming... like velvety chocolate cake or deep-dish apple pie. Something wonderful and of substance! So I just want people to see me there in that casket with a fork in my hand and I want them to wonder, 'What's with the fork?' Then I want you to tell them: 'Keep your fork... the best is yet to come.'

At the funeral people were walking by the woman's casket and they saw the pretty dress she was wearing and her favorite Bible and the fork placed in her right hand. Over and over, the pastor heard the question, "What's with the fork?" And over and over he smiled. During his message, the pastor told the people of the conversation he had with the woman shortly before she died. (author unknown)

She really got it – the Lord's words directed her life: "This is indeed the will of my Father, that all who see the Son and believe in him may have eternal life; and I will raise them up on the last day." He told them about the fork and what it symbolized to her. The pastor told the people how he could not stop thinking about the fork and told them that they probably would not be able to stop thinking about it either. He was right. So the next time you reach down for your fork, let it remind you that the best is yet to come.

A Long Bus Ride

A NEWSPAPER ACCOUNT reported the following incident.

A normal day turned into a frightening experience for a five-year-old child and his parents. The child was left on a school bus all day and was not discovered by the bus driver until around 3 p.m. "We put him on the bus at 6:25 a.m., and he was on the bus until the driver brought him home at 4:20 p.m.," said the mother of the five-year-old. When the child came home that day, he told his parents that he forgot to go to school!

Our Lord makes this promise – you will not be forgotten on the bus. Matter of fact, when your bus comes to its final stop, he will be the first in line to greet you. As the Lord takes your hand, his gentle voice will fill you with overwhelming love: "I've been waiting for you. Welcome home." Should our hearts become heavy and wearied over the final journey of our loved ones, hold on. We have this guarantee: "I will come again and will take you to myself, that where I am you may be also."

Avoid the Root Canals of Life

"PEACE I LEAVE WITH YOU; my peace I give to you. Not as the world gives do I give it to you. Do not let your hearts be troubled or afraid." How do we find this peace that Jesus wants us to experience? A peace that gets us through the root canals of life?

Maybe you need to make peace with yourself. Perhaps there are days when you are your own worst enemy. Here are 10 suggestions for embracing Christ's peace:

1. Don't nurse a grudge – it's a major factor in unhappiness.
2. Don't live in the past. A preoccupation with old mistakes
   and failures can lead to depression.
3. Don't waste time and energy fighting conditions you cannot change. Keep your focus on what you can influence.
4. Resist the temptation to withdraw and become reclusive during challenging times.
5. Don't indulge in self-pity. Accept that nobody gets through life without some sorrow and misfortune.
6. Don't expect too much of yourself. When there's too wide a gap between self-expectation and your ability to meet your goals, feelings of inadequacy will be inevitable.
7. Don't become self-absorbed. Find something bigger than yourself to believe in. Self-centered people score lowest in any test for measuring happiness.
8. Don't focus on what you have lost; focus on what you have left.
9. Don't compare yourself to others. You will become vain or bitter.
10. Don't pray in generalities. Ask for what you need and ask to do God's will.

Let his peace this day liberate you from situations that try to pull you under the surf. Trust that he can calm the waters.

Hold Onto the Vine

IN THE 1988 OLYMPICS the U.S. Men's Volleyball team made it to the semi-finals. One of the players, Bob Samuelson, cursed at a referee. The U.S. team was assessed one penalty point, which ultimately cost them the game and a chance at the Gold medal. The next day they returned to play for the Bronze medal. As the team took the court, many of the men had shaved their heads. You see, Bob Samuelson is bald, and they were saying, "He may have been wrong, but he is still our friend. He blew it, but he's still one of us and still on the team." Like the Olympic team, Jesus stands by us – so eager to accompany us along the way. The metaphor of the vine and branches is perfect in communicating God's desire to intimately share our lives.

Grapevines are so different from many plants. Take the banana plant. When a banana stalk is separated from the plant and placed in a hole and watered, it continues to live and will grow into a new plant. This new banana plant will produce much fruit. However, when a branch is removed from a grapevine, it cannot be replanted and grow into a new plant. It is useless. It dries up. This day take heart. Whether or not you feel worthy of God's love is unimportant – hold onto the Vine! Whether you've doubted or struggled with God is unimportant – hold onto the Vine! Since the world can snap us off so easily – hold onto the Vine! Remember that "He who abides in me, and I in him, he it is that bears much fruit, for apart from me you can do nothing."

The Only Move
You'll Ever Need to Know

SOMETIMES OUR BIGGEST weakness can become our biggest strength. A 10-year-old boy had decided to study judo although he had lost his left arm in a devastating car accident. The boy began lessons with an old Japanese judo master. The boy was doing well, so he couldn't understand why, after three months of training, the master had taught him only one move.

"Sensei," the boy finally said, "Shouldn't I be learning more moves?"

"This is the only move you know, but this is the only move you'll ever need to know," the sensei replied. Not quite understanding, but believing in his teacher, the boy kept training.

Several months later, the sensei took the boy to his first tournament. Surprising himself, the boy easily won his first two matches. The third match proved to be more difficult, but again he triumphed. In the final match, his opponent was bigger, stronger, and more experienced. For a while, the boy appeared to be overmatched. Concerned that the boy might get hurt, the referee called a time-out. He was about to stop the match when the sensei intervened. "No," the sensei insisted, "Let him continue." Soon after the match resumed, his opponent made a critical mistake: he dropped his guard. Instantly, the boy used his move to pin him. The boy had won the match and the tournament. He was the champion. On the way home, the boy and sensei reviewed every move in each and every match. Then the boy summoned the courage to ask what was really on his mind. "Sensei, how did I win the tournament with only one move?"

"You won for two reasons," the sensei answered. "First, you've almost mastered one of the most difficult throws in all of judo. And second, the only known defense for that move is for your opponent to grab your left arm." (author unknown)

The Holy Spirit, like the young boy's teacher, intercedes to guide, coach, and encourage us through the myriad of challenges in our lives. Sometimes we forget the promise or sometimes the promise just seems too good to be true. On the night before Jesus died, he announced, "I will ask the Father, and he will give you another Advocate to be with you always, the Spirit of truth" An advocate pleads our cause, takes our side, and conducts our defense. When we cannot pray, the Advocate prays within us. When we cannot save ourselves, the Advocate saves us and lifts us up. When we dare not approach the God we have offended by sin, the Advocate gives us confidence by speaking words of pardon and mercy. Today put your faith in the Holy Spirit. Let your spirit be uplifted. Ask him to intercede for you. And, where possible, intercede for those who rely on your voice to speak for them

A Gift to the Dead: A Hope to the Living

ON MAY 11, 1873, a 33-year-old Father Joseph Damien landed at Molokai, Hawaii. A disease-ridden crowd suffering from leprosy gathered at the landing. For more than a decade Damien would clean wounds, bandage ulcers, even amputate gangrenous limbs. Previously, the dead had been thrown in a ravine or buried in graves so shallow that wild pigs ravaged the corpses. Damien dug graves, built coffins, and said funeral Masses. It is estimated that he built more than 1,600 coffins during his years at Molokai. After 11 years it was evident that Damien had contracted leprosy. He persisted in his tireless activity until three weeks before his death. When those by his bedside grieved that he was leaving them orphaned, Damien replied: "Oh, no! If I have any credit with God, I'll intercede for everyone." On his tomb stone is engraved "Greater love hath no man than this, that a man lay down his life for his friends"

One of the greatest diseases, Mother Teresa tells us, is "to be nobody to anybody." Perhaps this day someone in your family, your work place, someone in your Church, at the hospital, in your neighborhood is feeling like a nobody. In the spirit of Blessed Damien, recognize the sacred spirit of that person and do something that affirms this person's worth.

Who Will Take the Son?

A WEALTHY MAN AND HIS SON loved to collect rare works of art. They had everything in their collection from Picasso to Raphael. When the Vietnam conflict broke out, the son went to war. He was very courageous and died in battle while rescuing another soldier. The father was notified and grieved deeply for his only son. About a month later, just before Christmas, there was a knock at the door. A young man stood at the door with a large package in his hands. He said, "Sir, you don't know me, but I am the soldier for whom your son gave his life. He saved many lives that day, and he was carrying me to safety when a bullet struck him in the heart, and he died instantly. He often talked about you, and your love for art." The young man held out his package. "I know this isn't much. I'm not really a great artist, but I think your son would have wanted you to have this." The father opened the package. It was a portrait of his son, painted by the young man. The father was so drawn to the eyes that his own eyes welled up with tears. He thanked the young man and offered to pay him for the picture. "Oh, no sir, I could never repay what your son did for me. It's a gift." The man died a few months later. There was to be a great auction of his paintings.

On the platform sat the painting of the son. The auctioneer pounded his gavel. "We will start the bidding with this picture of the son. Who will bid for this picture?" There was silence. Then a voice in the back of the room shouted, "We want to see the famous paintings. Skip this one." But the auctioneer persisted. "Will someone bid for this painting? Who will start the bidding? $100, $200?" Another voice shouted angrily, "We didn't come to see this painting. We came to see the Van Goghs, the Rembrandts. Get on with the real bids!" But still the auctioneer continued, "The son! The son! Who'll take the son?" Finally, a voice came from the very back of the room. It was the longtime gardener of the man and his son. "I'll give $10 for the painting." Being a poor man, it was all he could afford. "We have $10, who will bid $20?" "Give it to him for $10. Let's see the masters." "$10 is the bid, won't someone bid $20?" The crowd was becoming angry. They wanted the more worthy investments for their collections. The auctioneer pounded the gavel. "Going once, twice, SOLD FOR $10!"

A man sitting on the second row shouted, "Now, let's get on with the collection!" The auctioneer laid down his gavel. "I'm sorry, the auction is over." "What about the paintings?" "I am sorry. When I was called to conduct this auction, I was told of a secret stipulation in the will. I was not allowed to reveal that stipulation until this time. Only the painting of the son would be auctioned. Whoever bought that painting would inherit the entire estate, including the paintings. The man who took the son gets everything!" (author unknown)

Much like the auctioneer, God speaks to us "The Son, the Son, who'll take the Son?" Because whoever takes the Son gets everything. "For God so loved the world that he gave his only Son, so that everyone who believes in him may not perish but may have eternal life. "

Flat Tire

THE STORY IS TOLD of four high school boys who couldn't resist the temptation to skip morning classes. Each had been smitten with a bad case of spring fever. After lunch they showed up at school and reported to the teacher that their car had a flat tire. Much to their relief, she smiled and said, "Well, you missed a quiz this morning, so take your seats and get out a pencil and paper." Still smiling, she waited as they settled down and got ready for her questions. Then she said, "First question—which tire was flat?" (author unknown)

Truthfulness – easy to espouse this virtue, not so easy to live. Why? Sometimes we simply don't know how much truth to share in a given situation. Other times, it's just too demanding on our safety zones and requires too much personal risk. Our Lord comes to us with his compassionate heart. Today he asks you, "How can I help?" Do you know the answer to his question? Listen to his promise: When the Spirit of truth comes, he will guide you into all the truth...." May these words bring you insight, hope, and perseverance.

Suffering Should
Never Be Wasted

FR. JIM WILLING, a beloved priest from Cincinnati, Ohio, suffered excruciating pain as he battled cancer. Though Fr. Jim eventually succumbed to the disease, his unconquerable spirit continues to uplift others bearing through their illness. The following excerpts from his book *Lessons from the School of Suffering* speak to our Lord's promise that "your sorrow will turn into joy." Fr. Jim gives us insights for bringing meaning to our suffering, dealing with our demons, helping another when words fail, and taking the long view on suffering.

"What I want to say to every suffering person is that suffering should never be wasted. Never. The worst thing that could happen to us is not that we would suffer, but that we would waste our suffering or simply endure it. Instead, we should grow from it, and learn from it, and let it unite us to the Lord."

"We all have our "demons" that regularly trip us up….The demon is anything that "demeans" or hurts us or others in any way…. They seem to wait to attack, like enemies at battle, in our weakest times… when we are least able to fight back. It is helpful to realize how our demons have power over us….Therefore, we need to know what to do or where to go for help."

"Imagine the shape of each of your ears. If you were to join these two shapes together, you would have a perfect heart. The best way to share that heart, to love someone, is to listen to him or her."

"When I didn't know what to do or say, I would simply ask if I could offer a brief prayer for them. This is something we can all do for each other. Even though we may not know how to help someone, we can always be confident that God knows how to help the person."

"God always has an eternal view of what is best for us. For this reason God will allow suffering and hardship into our lives to prepare and purify us for life everlasting."

Farewell - Not Really

In some ways all of life is a letting go. It begins with the first loss you can remember through the most recent loss that flushes your soul with tears. Just as Jesus grieved for his friends as they spent their final days with him, he anguishes for us. Through his compassionate stare, he gives us great news: "So you have pain now; but I will see you again, and your hearts will rejoice, and no one will take your joy from you. On that day you will ask nothing of me." The destiny of our loved ones, the destiny for ourselves – to be protected from pain of body and spirit, embraced by the light of joy, and complete in every way. May the following words, shared at a mother's funeral, bring you comfort and hope in your day.

"I give you a promise that though I am home in the bosom of God, I am still present with you, whenever and wherever you call on me. My energy will be drawn to you by the magnet of our love. Whenever you are in need, call me; I will come to you with my arms full of wisdom and light to open up your blocked paths, to untangle your knots and to be your avenue to God. I have taken with me your love and the millions of memories of all that we have shared. So I have truly entered my new life as a millionaire. Fear not nor grieve my departure, you whom I have loved so much. For my roots and yours are forever intertwined." (Ed Hays)

The Stone and Its Force

THINKING BACK TO HIS CHILDHOOD, a man recalls a pivotal moment in his life.

My grandfather took me to the fish pond on the farm when I was about seven, and he told me to throw a stone into the water. He told me to watch the circles created by the stone. Then he asked me to think of myself as that stone. "You may create lots of splashes in your life but the waves that come from those splashes will disturb the peace of all your fellow creatures," he said. "Remember that you are responsible for what you put in your circle and that circle will also touch many other circles. You will need to live in a way that allows the good that comes from your circle to send the peace of that goodness to others. The splash that comes from anger or jealousy will send those feelings to other circles. You are responsible for both." That was the first time I realized each person creates the inner peace or discord that flows out into the world. We cannot create world peace if we are riddled with inner conflict, hatred, doubt, or anger. We radiate the feelings and thoughts that we hold inside, whether we speak them or not. Whatever is splashing around inside of us is spilling out into the world, creating beauty or discord with all other circles of life. Remember the eternal wisdom: "Whatever you focus on expands." (author unknown)

Think about what you are putting in your circle that will touch other circles? What do you need this day to keep negativity from taking over your circle? Sometimes it helps to take a breath and name your life treasures or simply to acknowledge a handful of benefits that bless your day. How many people will pass your path today? You could treat these encounters as routine happenings or as significant passings. Maybe it's only your smile, a caring hello, a sincere encouragement, a compassionate heart that simply listens – but this giving of yourself creates those circles that will touch so many others. Suddenly the everyday becomes an enthusiastic embrace of your day.

A Memorable Passing

A VETERINARIAN HAD BEEN CALLED to examine a ten-year old Irish Wolfhound named Belker. They were hoping for a miracle. Unfortunately the veterinarian determined that the dog was dying of cancer. Since there was nothing more the family could do for their beloved pet, the veterinarian offered to perform the euthanasia procedure for the old dog in the family's home. As arrangements were made, Ron and Lisa told the doctor they would like four-year old Shane to observe the procedure. They felt as though Shane might learn something from the experience. The next day, the veterinarian felt the familiar catch in his throat as Belker's family surrounded him. Shane seemed so calm, petting the old dog for the last time. Within a few minutes, Belker slipped peacefully away.

The little boy accepted Belker's transition without any difficulty or confusion. The doctor and Shane's parents wondered aloud about the sad fact that animal lives are shorter than human lives. Shane, who had been listening quietly, piped up, "I know why." The veterinarian had never heard a more comforting explanation. Shane said, "People are born so that they can learn how to live a good life — like loving everybody all the time and being nice, right?" The four-year-old continued, "Well, dogs already know how to do that, so they don't have to stay as long." (author unknown)

All of us look for comfort when death's shadow numbs our life. When the apostles finally understand that Jesus must die, sorrow fills their hearts. Yet Jesus gives them hope – an incredible promise of God's presence – a companion to be with them in their darkest moments. "It is to your advantage that I go away, for if I do not go away, the Advocate will not come to you; but if I go, I will send him to you." How many of us really grasp the power of the Holy Spirit; how many of us pray with expectation to "the Advocate."? Then the Advocate can direct us, breathe hope into hopeless situations, see our loved ones through their crossings and ultimately lead us to our eternal home.

Divine Interruption

FIVE YEAR OLD JOHNNY was in the kitchen as his mother made supper. She asked him to go into the pantry and get her a can of tomato soup. But he didn't want to go in alone. "It's dark in there and I'm scared." She asked again, and he persisted. Finally she said, "It's OK – Jesus will be in there with you." Johnny walked hesitantly to the door and slowly opened it. He peeked inside, saw it was dark, and started to leave when all at once an idea came, and he said: Jesus, if you're in there, would you hand me that can of tomato soup?" (author unknown)

When God breaks into our lives in unexpected ways, we feel confused and frightened – ready to tell Him to just hand us the tomato soup. Hearing the Christmas story over and over again, we can become desensitized to the shock Mary experiences when God breaks into her life. Mary expected to have an ordinary wedding with her ordinary fiancé and live an ordinary life. Gabriel took Mary by surprise. "She was much perplexed by his words and pondered what sort of greeting this might be." Gabriel doesn't ask Mary if this is a convenient time. He simply announces God's plan to break into the world through her. "The Holy Spirit will come upon you, and the power of the Most High will overshadow you; therefore the child to be born will be holy; he will be called Son of God." Mary's "yes" is the greatest statement of trust of all time. "Here am I, the servant of the Lord; let it be with me according to your word."

Like Mary, we can eventually embrace our own interruptions as a gift from God if we are convinced that God is behind the unexpected. Yet not every crisis entering our lives is sent by God. If our friends are going through a tragic interruption, be careful not to insist that their hardship is the will of God. We do not know that. And even if we would be right, people need to work through their perplexity and fear – before embracing their situation. If it is of God, then God will get them there.

Maybe our best role is to sit and wait with them. What we do know is that no interruption is greater than our God – and God can bring hope in the midst of any crisis or loss. We have no choice about the interruptions of life; they simply come to us. We can, however, choose to embrace them if we allow the Holy Spirit to do his creative work in us and through those we love. May we join our voice with Mary and announce, "Here am I, the servant of the Lord; let it be with me according to your word."

More than Enough

IT WASN'T MUCH, but in his hands it was more than enough. When Jesus sees the hungry crowd, he asks, "Where are we to buy bread for these people to eat?" Andrew spies the boy and offers his minimal solution. "There is a boy here who has five barley loaves and two fish. But what are they among so many people?"

We are not told anything about the youngster's background. Was he a little peddler, who thought that he could make some money by selling a few loaves and fishes? Perhaps the boy heard Andrew's skeptical comments about the futility of his meager offering. Maybe the boy wondered why he should surrender his food for the impossible need. What about himself? Maybe he would need that food to sustain his journey back home.

But the young boy sacrifices to help Jesus nourish the crowd. As Jesus receives the small gift and feeds the thousands, the standing of that lad is transformed. He matters; his gift matters. The young boy likely sees himself in a new light. Perhaps Jesus would like to borrow something from us: maybe our compassion, our voice for the needy, our gift for drawing, writing, counting; maybe our time – maybe we can offer a meal, babysit, or bring laughter to the burdened. Alone our gift may be insignificant. But combined with the power of Christ's love, we can be an influence for tremendous good.

The End or Is It?

FIFTY YEARS IN THE SAME old farm house. And now the end was near. Opal sat in the worn lawn chair. Strangers stepped past her, looking through the "stuff" of her life. The auctioneer's voice wooed the people closer to her belongings – soon to be their belongings. With the final purchase made and the auctioneer paid, Opal would say her goodbye. Though she had time to anticipate the ending, she could feel the emptiness causing her to shake. What would become of her rose bushes, of the beans and cucumbers in the garden? Who would keep the paint crisp on Bud's garage? Within a few weeks, a young family moved into Opal's home. The lilac bushes surrendered to a chain link fence. The grand maple tree was overpowered by industrial saws. Opal did pretty well for a while at the assisted living facility. But in the sixth month, she suffered a terminal stroke.

Opal's story is our story. Life is indeed a series of letting go. Eric Fromm raises a haunting question: "If I am what I have and if what I have is lost, who then am I?" Though we may fight the brutal reality, it's inevitable that we will lose everything. Or will we? Yes, the material essence of this world, but not the essence of eternal love and eternal life. Our Lord cautions us "not to work for the food that perishes." Instead to work for "food that endures for eternal life, which the Son of Man will give you." Jesus knew loss. You name it; he suffered it. Whatever loss burdens your day, a compassionate God accompanies you. You may not feel it; you may really doubt this. But the promise continues. And continues with no end.

"Purdy and Big"

ROB CUTSHAW OWNS A LITTLE roadside shop outside Andrews, North Carolina. Like many in the trade, he hunts for rocks, then sells them to collectors or jewelry makers. He knows enough about rocks to decide which to pick up and sell, but he's no expert. He leaves the appraising of his rocks to other people. While on a dig twenty years ago, Rob found a rock he described as "purdy and big." He tried unsuccessfully to sell the specimen. Rob guessed the blue chunk could bring as much as $500 dollars. He would have taken less if something urgent came up.

That's how close Rob came to hawking for a few hundred dollars what turned out to be the largest, most valuable sapphire ever found. The blue rock that Rob had abandoned to the darkness of a closet two decades ago—now known as "The Star of David" sapphire—weighs nearly a pound, and could easily sell for $2.75 million. *The Atlanta Journal Constitution,* May 17, 1987

Jesus has placed before us our blue rock – we can either hide it in the closet or recognize its astonishing value. Our Lord does not say, "I am sort of like the bread that comes down from heaven." Nor does he say, "You could think of me as if I were the bread of life if that would work for you as a spiritual metaphor."

No! Jesus states, "I am the bread of life." If Almighty God chose to reveal himself through the ordinary – a young girl and her baby – why wouldn't he choose the ordinary – bread and wine – to gift us with his very own presence? The next time you receive the Eucharist, trust in the incredible love of God. Trust that Jesus intimately joins you to fulfill the special calling he has entrusted to you.

The Great Lesson

TO ENCOURAGE HER YOUNG SON'S progress on the piano, a mother took the small boy to a Paderewski concert. After they were seated, the mother spotted a friend in the audience and walked down the aisle to greet her. Seizing the opportunity to explore the wonders of the concert hall, the little boy rose and eventually explored his way through a door marked: "NO ADMITTANCE."

When the house lights dimmed, and the concert was about to begin, the mother returned to her seat and discovered that her son was missing. Suddenly, the curtains parted and spotlights focused on the impressive Steinway on stage. In horror, the mother saw her little boy sitting at the keyboard, innocently picking out "Twinkle, Twinkle Little Star."

At that moment, the great piano master made his entrance, quickly moved to the piano, and whispered in the boy's ear, "Don't quit. Keep playing." Then leaning over, Paderewski reached down with his left hand and began filling in a bass part. Soon his right arm reached around to the other side of the child and he added a running obbligato. Together, the old master and the young novice transformed a frightening situation into a wonderfully creative experience. The audience was mesmerized. (anonymous)

That's the way it is with God. What we can accomplish on our own is hardly noteworthy. We try our best, but the results aren't exactly graceful flowing music. But with the hand of the Master, our life's work truly can be beautiful. Recall our Lord's words, "Very truly, I tell you, whoever receives one whom I send receives me; and whoever receives me receives him who sent me." Next time you set out to accomplish great feats, listen carefully. You can hear the voice of the Master whispering in your ear, "Don't quit. Keep playing." Feel his loving arms around you. Know that his strong hands are playing the concerto of your life. Remember, God doesn't call the equipped, he equips the called. Is he calling you to a special assignment? Trust that he will "play your piano with you."

It Could Have Been So Different

ONE SUMMER NIGHT during a severe thunderstorm a mother was tucking her small son into bed. She was about to turn the light off when he asked in a trembling voice, "Mommy, will you stay with me all night?" Smiling, the mother gave him a warm, reassuring hug and said tenderly, "I can't dear. I have to sleep in Daddy's room." A long silence followed. At last it was broken by a shaky voice saying, "The big sissy!" (author unknown)

The disciples, huddled in the upper room, eyes fixed on the locked door, probably felt like "big sissies"—especially when the figure of Jesus entered the room. Imagine if Jesus wanted to chastise them for ditching him. He could have shamed those apostles; he could have tortured their frightened spirits. Pretend that he was a ghost -back to haunt them for their betrayal. His opening words might have been, "Cowards, you did nothing to stop the scourge from ripping away my flesh. You losers!"

Instead, Jesus put his followers at ease; he shares his peace with them and humanizes his appearance. He calls them forward to touch his wounds; he partakes of the ordinary – the eating of a meal. How fitting that Jesus then encourages his followers to preach repentance and forgiveness to all nations. Mercy was not just a nice word to toss into their future sermons. Mercy lifted those apostles out of their depression; renewed their self-worth; and fortified them to carry the message of Christ's love to all people. So many opportunities to be his voice in our daily lives – yet sometimes we, too, choose the "sissy" route and lack the necessary solidarity with his Spirit. Do you need a stronger backbone for the conflicts you need to address; do you need to be tough so others can be true? Then do it. Know that his peace will lift you up when the rigor of the situation circles about you.

Has Anyone Seen the Pony?

Two boys were twins, one an incurable optimist, one a pessimist. The parents were worried about the extremes of behavior and attitude and finally took the boys in to see a psychologist. The psychologist observed them a while and then said that they could be easily helped. He said that they had a room filled with all the toys a boy could want. They would put the pessimist in that room and allow him to enjoy life. They also had another room that they filled with horse manure. They put the optimist in that room.

They observed both boys through one way mirrors. The pessimist continued to be a pessimist, stating that he had no one to play with. They went to look in on the optimist, and were astounded to find him digging through the manure. The psychologist ran into the room and asked what on earth the boy was doing. He replied that with all that manure, he was sure there had to be a pony in the room somewhere. (author unknown)

Because Jesus takes the ordinary moments of our day and breathes his life into them, we, too, can be optimists. Remember the fishing trip that wears down the apostles – the fish just aren't biting. Jesus calls to the men, "You have no fish, have you?" They answered him, "No." He said to them, "Cast the net to the right side of the boat, and you will find some." No dramatic shaking of the earth; no meteors zipping through the skies; not even the old days of walking on the water. Jesus meets the seven men where life is challenging them – in their boat with an empty net.

The risen Lord comes through. He blesses the fishermen with a catch of 153 fish. The Son of God, who has just conquered death, proceeds to cook a meal for the hungry men. Jesus doesn't even wait for the men to come to him; he brings the fish and bread to them. Astounding! The Lord of Lords serves his followers again. Today let us be that servant leader through the attitude we bring to the office meeting, to the people who bring us a meal and ring up our purchase; to the task of folding the laundry, buying the groceries, and in helping a child with homework. Sometimes it doesn't take much to be Christ to another. Mother Teresa reminds us, "We shall never know all the good that a simple smile can do." And by the way, if you're wondering if a pony is near by, that's not all bad – I bet those fishermen wondered about the fish. And we know the rest of that story!

God Didn't Really Mean It, Did He?

JUDITH WAS TYPICALLY a positive person. But when she brought up John, her ex-husband, look out! There was one story in particular that epitomized John's clueless vision of marriage. When the marriage therapist asked John how he knew that he loved Judith, he responded, "I take out the garbage for her every week, don't I!" Not too long after that John found himself taking out the garbage just for himself.

A few years after the divorce, however, something changed – or someone changed. Judith had a revelation – a divine revelation. She told her friends, "Last week I was thinking back to all the rotten things about John. Then it hit me. It was like a voice whispered to me. 'God loves John as much as he loves you.' I didn't want to hear that voice. Matter of fact, it almost made me nauseated. God just couldn't love John as much as me. Not if God had any sense. But then I admitted God had eternal sense. The voice was right." Scripture tells us that God "gives the Spirit without measure." Not more to your friends and less to those who bother you. Why? Because God's love is total for each of us. May this reality help us be less spiteful, more patient, and even more forgiving.

The Weather Vane's Truth

ONE DAY C. H. SPURGEON, a renowned preacher, was walking through the English countryside with a friend. The evangelist noticed a barn with a weather vane on its roof. At the top of the vane were these words: GOD IS LOVE. Spurgeon found the location for such words to be utterly inappropriate. "Weather vanes are changeable," he said, "but God's love is constant."

"I don't agree with you about those words," replied his friend. "You misunderstood the meaning. That sign is indicating a truth: Regardless of which way the wind blows, God is love." (author unknown)

For the adulterous woman brought before Jesus, horrific winds cut across her pathway. She gasps for breath as she readies herself for execution by stoning. How could an exit strategy exist for her? The pronouncement is made: "Teacher, this woman was caught in the very act of committing adultery. Now in the law Moses commanded us to stone such women. Now what do you say?"

She asks herself how this Jesus can possible save her. No loophole in her behavior; Caught red handed; barbaric rocks certain to brutalize her. But Jesus changes the course of the winds. "Let anyone among you who is without sin be the first to throw a stone at her." He bends down and writes on the ground and soon he is left alone with the woman standing before him. Could it be that the accusers themselves have committed sins deserving of stoning?

Jesus' comments to the woman are brief and affirming: "Woman, where are they? Has no one condemned you?" She said, "No one, sir." And Jesus said, "Neither do I condemn you. Go your way, and from now on do not sin again." How encouraging for each of us. Even when our wayward direction is really off course, we are invited back on path – accept forgiveness and start anew—not tomorrow but "from now on."

Waiting to Enter the Pool

WILL ROGERS WAS KNOWN for his laughter, but he also knew how to weep. One day he was entertaining at a hospital that specialized in rehabilitating polio victims and people with broken backs and other extreme physical handicaps. Of course, Rogers had everybody laughing, even patients in really bad condition; but then he suddenly left the platform and went to the rest room. A hospital administrator followed Rogers. When the administrator opened the door, he saw Will Rogers leaning against the wall, sobbing like a child. In a few minutes, Rogers appeared back on the platform, as jovial as before. If you want to learn what a person is really like, ask two questions: What makes him laugh? What makes him weep? (author unknown)

Jesus also found himself in the company of a "multitude of invalids, blind, lame, paralyzed." In particular, one man had been ill for thirty-eight years and desperately wanted to be cured by the healing pool. At first glance Jesus seems to pose an insensitive question to the man. "Do you want to be healed?" No doubt this man had agonized watching others be healed. He waited and waited but it was not his turn, not today, not tomorrow.

Perhaps Jesus knew that the man's healing would demand a total change in lifestyle. If cured, his life would offer many new choices. Perhaps he could be the eyes, the legs, the voice for those who stared with futility at the waters. Just as he had wept for himself, now he might weep for those waiting their chance to enter the miraculous waters. And just as his physical freedom brought laughter, now he could celebrate the cures of others. Do we want to be healed? Then we must be willing to turn our sorrow into our servant? Are we ready to focus not on what we have lost, but on what we have left? If we are to be healed, we must grow in patience. We don't know if our turn will come to enter the pool. But we do know our highest good is the Lord's plan for us.

Finger Tips On Hope

MAMIE MADE FREQUENT TRIPS to the branch post office. One day she confronted a long line of people who were waiting for service from the postal clerks. Mamie only needed stamps, so a helpful observer asked, "Why don't you use the stamp machine? You can get all the stamps you need and you won't have to stand in line." Mamie said, "I know, but the machine can't ask me about my arthritis." People still need human contact. (author unknown)

Human contact – Jesus yearned for human contact as he prepared for his death. He gathered his friends together for his last meal; later he would ask them to wait and pray as he anguished over his imminent death. They were too tired to remember him; he was too true to abandon them. They knew betrayal; he knew bottomless forgiveness. We can understand a Pharisee betraying Jesus; that's expected. But a trusted friend; someone who witnessed the Lord's compassion to so many; who traveled in the inner circle, who experienced the divine power and the divine love. No one suspected Judas. Why would they? He protected their collective monies. He never spoke of his dissatisfaction with Jesus; never hinted that he would leave the group. Now Judas is told, "What you are going to do, do quickly." Then there's Peter. "Lord, why cannot I follow you now? I will lay down my life for you." Jesus answered, "Will you lay down your life for me? Truly, truly, I say to you, the cock will not crow, till you have denied me three times." Why does Jesus bluntly tell Peter that his promise is useless; that Peter will betray his Lord not once, not twice, but three times?

Jesus wants Peter to remember this prediction so Peter will not lose heart after he betrays the Lord. Even though Jesus knew this outcome, he showed Peter his unconditional love. How? He still chose Peter to witness his agony in the garden – to see him so vulnerable and to follow from afar as the crucifixion neared. Judas despairs and hangs himself. Peter keeps his finger tips on hope. He trusts more in the Lord's mercy than his own weakness. Let this be our lesson. His mercy triumphs over our failings, even when we fail again and again.

A Lavish Expression of Love

A BUSINESSMAN KNOWN for his ruthless practices bragged to Mark Twain, "Before I die I mean to make a pilgrimage to the Holy Land. I will climb Mount Sinai and read the 10 Commandments aloud at the top." Twain retorted, "I have a better idea. You could stay in Boston and keep them."

Judas Iscariot, like this businessman, feigns superior morality. For Judas, his objections to Mary's expensive anointing of Jesus' feet provide the subterfuge for his plan to betray Jesus. But Mary doesn't care about the accusations by Judas. Her focus is upon her Lord; she loves him completely; she must seize her time with him before the traitor executes his plan. Mary lavishly pours the ointment on Jesus' feet, ointment that cost over a year's salary. She takes the pins from her pristine hair; moves her head downward and dries the feet of Jesus. It is her demonstrative and lavish expression of love. Mary feels compelled to give her Lord the best of her possessions, to use her beauty to show her homage, and to make herself vulnerable to Judas' derogatory words. Jesus defends Mary to him: "Leave her alone. She bought it so that she might keep it for the day of my burial. You always have the poor with you, but you do not always have me." Of course Mary's compassion for the poor has been a constant. But now she must give herself completely to the Lord.

Dag Hammarskjold, Noble Peace Prize recipient, speaks to Mary's behavior. "It is more noble to give yourself completely to one individual than to labor diligently for the salvation of the masses." Take inventory today. Learn from Mary. Love the Lord lavishly; love the one completely; and your impact on the many will be monumental.

Washing the Dirt
from Between the Toes

LET'S CALL HIM CHARLES. In Mother Teresa's Prescription, Dr. Paul Wright, a Notre Dame Cardiologist, describes an unusual encounter with an older psychiatrist. "One day, he invited me to his house. He lived alone, and the first thing I noticed in his house were the many squares on the wallpaper where frames had once hung. I asked Charles where the pictures had gone and he took me to his basement door."

"He had removed all his degrees, honorary degrees, and award certificates from their frames, folded them into a paper airplane, and flew them down the basement stairs, one by one. He tried to fling each one farther than the last. It had become a game for him."

Why had Charles done this? Dr. Wright came to learn that "these symbols of power and prestige came to mean nothing to him. His drive to obtain them had caused him much personal loss. His focus on work and materialistic advantages, titles, and prestige had cost him his wife and children many years earlier. In the end, he also lost his professional prestige and relationships that had kept him in good standing in the medical community."

In later years Dr. Wright came to more fully understand the significance of this encounter. "Be careful, control your ego and your desire for power, recognition, and authority. If you don't it will control and destroy the things that matter in your life and will ultimately destroy you." Specifically how could Charles have escaped this downfall and celebrated a life of abundance? Jesus demonstrates his answer at the Last Supper. Remember the scene? He is bent down washing the dirt from the toes of his apostles, even the toes of Judas. Does this boggle your mind? It should. The creator of the universe, who knows every thought of every creature from all time, and configures all of life and all of death, removes the dust from crevices of his followers' feet. Jesus explains: "So if I, your Lord and Teacher, have washed your feet, you also ought to wash one another's feet. For I have set you an example, that you also should do as I have done to you."

As you judge your success today – ask this question that Jesus poses to you. "Did you find the wash basin and towel? Did you clean the feet of those whose shoes aren't as nice as yours? Whose jobs aren't as "important" as yours? Who are younger than you, or who are closer to one final sunrise. Great! You get it. You really get it!"

Leave the Rest to Me

As a man was climbing the stairs of the lighthouse, he carried a small candle. On the man's way up to the top, the candle spoke up, "Where are we going?"

"We're going to the top of this lighthouse to signal the big ships on the ocean," the man answered. "What? How could it be possible for me with my small light to give signals to those big ships?"

"They will never be able to see my light," bemoaned the candle. "That's your part. If your light is small, let it be. All you have to do is keep burning and leave the rest to me," said the man. A little later, they arrived at the top of the lighthouse where there was a big lamp with a loop behind it. The man lit the lamp with the light of the candle and instantly, the place shone so brightly that the ships on the ocean could see its light.

Jesus tells the Pharisees "even if you do not believe me, believe the works, so that you may know and understand that the Father is in me and I am in the Father." Have you ever looked closely at a flame? Glowing within the apparent flame is the inner one that seems to give power to the visible tongue of fire. The eternal flame of Christ's love unites with our small efforts to bring forth expansive light.

Even if your light is small or dim, if you trust all your life to God, he is able to make your small light into a magnificent one that brings blessings to many people. If we believe more in the power of his love than in our own weakness, we can achieve great things. Tap into the divine synergy that brought hope to the lost, healing to the sick, and brought Jesus from the agony in the garden to the triumph of the cross.

Who is Building the House?

FOUR ROYAL BROTHERS decided each to master a special ability. Time went by and the brothers met to reveal their special gift. "I have mastered a science," said the first, "by which I can take but a bone of some creature and create the flesh that goes with it." The second brother boasted that he knew "how to grow that creature's skin and hair if there is flesh on its bones." The next brother announced that he was "able to create its limbs if the flesh, the skin, and the hair exited." And the fourth brother stood tall when he proclaimed that he knew "how to give life to that creature if its form is complete."

Then the brothers went into the jungle to find a bone so they could demonstrate their specialties. As fate would have it, the bone they found was a lion's. One added flesh to the bone, the second grew hide and hair, the third completed it with matching limbs, and the fourth gave the lion life. Shaking its mane, the ferocious beast arose and jumped on his creators. He killed them all and vanished contentedly into the jungle. (author unknown)

The story underscores the following lesson. Unless we first seek God's kingdom and allow Him to breathe his life into it, we, too, have the capacity to create what can devour us. Mother Teresa extends this warning even to our apparent good deeds. "I am not sure exactly what heaven will be like, but I do know that when we die and it comes time for God to judge us, he will NOT ask, how many good things have you done in your life. Rather he will ask how much LOVE did you put into what you did."

Jesus reminds his critics that his behavior is motivated by the glory he brings to his Father. "If I glorify myself, my glory is nothing." Mother Teresa cautions us to be clear about our motivation – good deeds that originate from selfish intentions miss the essence of Christ's call to serve. Those we help then can simply become objects to further our own gain. Always remember "Unless the Lord builds the house, they labor in vain that build it."

Ask our Lord's spirit to be the driving motivation in your life. Today slowly pray the words of St. Ignatius: "Take, Lord, and receive all my liberty, my memory, my understanding, and my entire will, all that I have and possess. Thou hast given all to me. To Thee, O Lord, I return it. All is Thine, dispose of it wholly according to Thy will. Give me Thy love and Thy grace, for this is sufficient for me."

The Panel of Roses

THE AMERICAN PAINTER, John Sargent, once painted a panel of roses that received the highest praise from the critics. Though a small picture, it approached perfection. On several occasions Sargeant was offered a great deal of money for his painting, yet he always refused to sell to the buyers. Why? Whenever he was deeply discouraged and doubtful of his abilities as an artist, he would look at the panel of roses and remind himself, "I painted that." Then he would reclaim his confidence and go forward with his projects.

How helpful it would be if we had our panel of roses – a reminder that God has given us just the gifts we need to find satisfaction; an assurance that wayward times will finally end; a promise that confusion will eventually earn us interior direction. Jesus does offer that panel of roses. He tells us, "If you continue in my word, you are truly my disciples; and you will know the truth, and the truth will make you free." What truth is evading you today? Something about your future, you family, your health, a tough decision – maybe you've been rationalizing your behavior and truth is tugging at you.

Have you asked our Lord to inspire you with the truth? It's not easy to walk through the door of truth. But once you cross the threshold, the freedom promised you will permeate all facets of your life. Stop waiting. Walk across.

Why Didn't He Tell You Sooner?

IN DECEMBER OF 1903, after many attempts, the Wright brothers were successful in getting their "flying machine" off the ground. Thrilled, they telegraphed this message to their sister Katherine: "We have actually flown 120 feet. Will be home for Christmas." Katherine hurried to the editor of the local newspaper and showed him the message. He glanced at it and said, "How nice. The boys will be home for Christmas." He totally missed the big news- man had flown! *(Our Daily Bread)*

Missing the big news – doesn't that sound like the disciples on their way to Emmaus. They must have wondered "what's the point?" Why should the followers of the crucified Jesus hang out in Jerusalem? The third day had come. The promise was broken. Try and forget. Move on. Get out of Jerusalem – at least Emmaus would be safer. So Cleopas and his friend begin their seven mile walk, a journey of two hours. The two men invite a third into their company. The stranger soon asks the most out of touch question about the happenings of the weekend. Aggravated, Cleopus answers, "Are you the only stranger in Jerusalem who does not know the things that have taken place there in these days?" Jesus responds, "What things?"

Imagine the future conversation Cleopas and his friend might share with their families – telling them about this stranger. Certainly someone must have asked, "Why didn't he tell you upfront who he was?" "Best that he didn't tell us. We spent a good three miles learning about the fulfillment of the Old Testament from the teacher. Now I finally get it. All ages have waited for this moment."

"You know, he wanted to keep on his journey, but we insisted that he dine with us. Thank goodness because here's the most amazing part. When he broke bread with us, we knew it was Jesus. I really believe we will never be alone. Our Lord will always be present in the breaking of the bread."

Look for his disguised presence right now. Do you need to reach out a little more? Do it. What if Cleopas and his friend had not gone the extra: Remember how they "constrained Jesus saying to him 'Stay with us, for it is toward evening and the day is now spent.' And he went in to stay with them." This was a simple act of kindness; a singular moment of divine love!

Look for the Nail Prints

DURING THE MIDDLE AGES a popular story circulated about Martin of Tours. It was said that Satan once appeared to St Martin in the guise of the Savior himself. St. Martin was ready to fall to his feet and worship this resplendent being of glory and light. Then, suddenly, he looked up into the palms of his hands and asked, "Where are the nail prints?" Whereupon the apparition vanished.

Our Lord is both resplendent being and being riveted by nails. In John's Gospel, Jesus foretells the comingling of his nature: "When you have lifted up the Son of Man, then you will realize that I am he." The Pharisees just don't get it. "Who are you?" resonates in their shouts and whispers. Jesus, irritated by their arrogance and hypocrisy, answers "Why do I speak to you at all?"

The early church leader Augustine understood our Lord's frustration. When a non-believer accosted Augustine by displaying his idol and boasting, "Here is my god; where is thine?" Augustine replies, "I cannot show you my God; not because there is no God to show, but because you have no eyes to see." How will you know if you see God today? Let's ask the question another way? What can you count on just for this day? There you shall see God!

To Everyone's Surprise

A CHINESE WOMAN was leading the other athletes in the last phase of the women's 10 mile walk event at the Olympics. The distance she had covered in her training was enough to travel the globe a few times. Now a Gold Medal was in view. While she was entering the stadium, she noticed another athlete quickly coming from behind. She desperately wanted to go faster but was unable to do so without having both her feet leave the ground. Such a movement would constitute running – an infraction against the rules. Anyone found "running" three times would be disqualified.

The front runner remembered she had violated this rule twice in the past nine miles. She was tempted but persisted in keeping her feet down. Soon the woman saw the other athlete over take her. A Gold turned Silver. A while later, another athlete came from behind and passed her. A Silver turned Bronze. The first athlete past the finished line and the crowd roared. The second athlete past the finished line and there was a big applause. The Chinese athlete finished third with much disappointment. All these years of hard work only to end with a Bronze Medal. When the official of the game announced the winner, to everyone's surprise, the Gold Medal went to the Chinese athlete. The two athletes before her had violated the rule of running in a walk event. (author unknown)

Who is our judge? Who sets the rules of our lives? Do you feel like the gold is slipping away, and you are trying to do right? It's not easy to persevere when the race doesn't seem to be going our way. Yet when did our Lord say, "Sign up with me. It will be a cake walk?" That was never in the contract. Jesus reminds us what matters most – follow him. Speaking of his relationship with his Father, Jesus tells us that he seeks "to do not my own will but the will of him who sent me." What does this mean for us in practical terms? Today think about the following questions as you join your will with his divine will.

- Do I want to grow where He wants me to grow?
- How can I use my adversity to become more

compassionate, less judgmental, and more trusting of His love?

- Do I want to change where he wants me to change?
- Do I want to cease being what he does not want me to be?

Through it all – we are promised the Gold. Hold to that belief today!

God's Portrait

A KINDERGARTEN TEACHER asked a boy what he was drawing. Without pausing to look up, he said, "A picture of God." The teacher smiled and responded, "But nobody knows what God looks like." The boy carefully put down his crayon, looked her squarely in the eye, and declared, "After I'm finished here they will." (author unknown)

How does God look to you? One image is found in his name – Emmanuel – God with us. Not God above us or adjacent to us – Not God on a business trip, or stuck in a traffic jam or skiing in the Rockies. But God with us now and always – in the routine of our day, in the rugged moments, in the relaxing escapes from the day's tension. He doesn't put conditions on being with us. "I'm with you if you never screw up, if you learn how to parent right, if you lose 15 pounds, if you make me look good to the skeptic." Instead our Lord is with us because "I have not come on my own...I am from him, and he sent me." The Father could have sent the "B" Team – Angels and Prophets. But, that wouldn't do. Too antiseptic – too removed from the barn odor and the beam's blood. Remember he's in your office, on your phone conversations, packing the kids' lunches, driving your car, or going to class. What more can we ask!

Expect To Hear From Him

THE STORY IS TOLD of Franklin Roosevelt, who often endured long receiving lines at the White House. He complained that no one really paid any attention to what was said. One day, during a reception, he decided to try an experiment. To each person who came down the line and shook his hand, he murmured, "I murdered my grandmother this morning." The guests responded with phrases like, "Marvelous! Keep up the good work. We are proud of you. God bless you, sir." It was not till the end of the line, while greeting the ambassador from Bolivia, that his words were actually heard. Nonplussed, the ambassador leaned over and whispered, "I'm sure she had it coming." (source unknown)

Like the people in Roosevelt's receiving line, we sometimes don't hear the obvious. Concerned about our own impression, convinced that we are right, or self-preoccupation can silence the other's voice. Fortunately Mary Magdalene knew how to listen—especially when her name was called.

Last at the cross, Mary Magdalene is first at the tomb. Rabbinic tradition held that mourning for the dead was at its greatest on the third day. Mary's grief is intense. She hopes that closeness to the grave will somehow ease the separation. Grief beyond grief blinds Mary to the presence of the angels. Even when she looks at Jesus, she cannot see him. Mary expects to find a corpse; she does not expect to see the living Christ. But then it happens. He calls her by name. At that instant Mary knows that the crucified Lord lives. Jesus assures her that "I am ascending to my Father and your Father, to my God and your God."

We, too, belong to the inner circle of divine love. Do you believe that the Lord calls you by name? Not some abstract invitation; more like the phone call of someone who treasures hearing your voice. Someone who just wants you to know they care; someone just checking in;

someone asking you to join them for a special event. Let's learn from Mary. When dreams fall apart, when loss knocks us down, listen for his voice. Take comfort. Expect to hear from him. He is near.

Checkmate?

PAUL MORPHY WAS THE world's champion chess player when he was invited by a friend to look at a valuable painting titled, "The Chess Player." In the painting, Satan was represented as playing chess with a young man, the stake being the young man's soul. The game had reached the stage where it was the young man's move; but he was checkmated. There was no move he could make which would not mean defeat for him and so the strong feature of the picture was the look of utter despair on the young man's face as he realized that his soul was lost.

Morphy, who knew more about chess than the artist, studied the picture for a time, then called for a chessboard and pieces. Placing them in exactly the same position as they were in the painting, he said, "I'll take the young man's place and make the move." Then he made the move which would have set the young man free. (author unknown)) Ever think of the Lord as the preeminent chess player? If today you're staring at the metaphorical chess board and you don't see the next move — that's okay. Trust him; trust yourself. Be patient. Remember who is helping you. Jesus speaks of the "works that the father has given me to complete," works which "testify on my behalf that the Father has sent me." We are his incomplete work, made more real and relevant through the checkmate moments of our lives. Keep this thought in mind: Our Lord has never surrendered to a checkmate yet. That's pretty good odds!

His Final Words - "More Weight"

A SMALL GIRL FELL SICK IN 1692. Her "fits"—convulsions, contortions, and outbursts of gibberish—baffled everyone. Other girls soon manifested the same symptoms. Their doctor could suggest but one cause – witchcraft. That grim diagnosis launched an inquisition that took 25 lives, filled prisons with innocent people, and frayed the soul of a Massachusetts community called Salem. An innocent man, Giles Corey, refused to plead innocent or guilty. He knew that by keeping his mouth shut, his estate would not be forfeited to the colony after his death. Although he had already signed over his farm to his sons-in-law, this transaction would not keep the government from seizing his property after they hanged him. If Giles died in prison without pleading, the authorities could not touch his property.

On September 17, Giles was led by the Sheriff to a field in Salem near the jail. He was stripped of his clothing, forced into a pit where boards were placed on his chest. Heavy stones were placed one at a time onto the prisoner's chest and stomach. The witnesses waited for a plea. None came. This went on for two days. Interrogators asked Giles on three separate occasions to plead one way or the other, innocent or guilty. But Giles simply replied "More weight". Corey is often seen as a martyr who "gave back fortitude and courage rather than spite and bewilderment." His public death played a role in building public opposition to the witchcraft trials.

Many people who brought claims of witchcraft against the innocent were motivated by greed, envy or fear—not unlike the scribes of Jesus' day. The religious leaders announced to the crowds that Jesus "has Beelzebul, and by the ruler of the demons he casts out demons." It's inconceivable that anyone would accuse Jesus of aligning with Satan, but they did! How does Jesus respond? He denounced the illogic of their statement and warned "whoever blasphemes against the Holy Spirit can never have forgiveness, but is guilty of an eternal sin."

Perhaps there were apostles or bystanders who defended Jesus—but no such voices are recorded. Throughout this day, there will be opportunities to be loyal to our Lord – to stand for him without embarrassment or apology. Maybe a co-worker, a brother or sister, a friend, etc, is experiencing unfair criticism or treatment. To be loyal to our Lord is to be loyal to the falsely accused. If we are unwilling to face the disapproval and rejection that might occur if we defend another, then we surrender our integrity for the hollow shell of popularity. If this day you also experience the slings and arrows of unkind words, take a deep breath. And fill up on the love of the Holy Spirit – our constant source of protection and guidance.

Fr. Hesburgh
and Famous Last Words

SOMEONE ONCE ASKED FR. HESBURGH, "If you were dying "what would you tell people?"

'I guess I'd most simply say, Love God and love each other. You can't imagine a world going wrong if it were full of people who love God and love each other and act accordingly... Good deeds done and good thoughts thought and carried out. Good efforts fortified in the lives of others. Giving, giving, giving, and yet always being happy to be able to give.

"Somehow I guess what it all boils down to is being what God wants us to be—a loving, caring people who know what loving is and know what caring is. And know what needs to be done to create a world of peace rather than a world of war and strife and hardship and suffering. We all have a part in that act. Nobody here that isn't... what they call a "dramatis persona"— the people in the drama. We're all in the drama.'"

And the Moon
Went on Shining

A JUDGE HAD BEEN RIDICULED frequently by a conceited lawyer. When asked by a friend why he didn't rebuke his assailant, he replied, "In our town lives a widow who has a dog. And whenever the moon shines, it goes outside and barks all night." Having said that, the magistrate shifted the conversation to another subject. Finally someone asked, "But Judge, what about the dog and the moon?" "Oh," he replied, "the moon went on shining—that's all." (author unknown)

Like the moon, we need to keep on shining when others malign us; when our good effort is twisted and our motives are leveled by other's insecurity and selfishness. Of course, if the criticism is true, we need to mend our ways. Otherwise, forget about it! Over and over again Jesus experiences the barking dog. Even when he restores health to the sick, he is accused of following Satan. 'He casts out demons by Beelzebul, the ruler of the demons.' In one encounter, Jesus calls upon his Father to drive out Satan from a tortured man. Our Lord brings optimal healing – sanity is restored, spiritual wholeness instilled, and the man reclaims his voice.

But jealousy grips the crowd. This healing should have been a magnificent moment – one where our Lord receives gratitude and reverence. Instead malicious accusations filter through the crowd. Jesus could not control what other's thought of him; however, he could control his choice to follow the path of his Father's will. If you find yourself unfairly accused or maligned, ask the Lord to protect you from the stress and anger that can accompany such treatment. Trust yourself. Keep moving in the direction of what's right. Stand up for yourself. Our Lord will stand up with you and for you!

How Much Difference Would It Make?

HENRY FORD WAS VACATIONING in Ireland when he was asked to contribute toward a new orphanage. Ford wrote a check for two thousand pounds. Although the gift made the headlines, the newspaper had mistakenly reported the gift as twenty thousand pounds. The director of the orphanage apologized to Ford. "There's no need for that," Ford replied, and immediately wrote a check for the additional eighteen thousand pounds. Such character and such compassion! An action that expresses true humanity.

Our Lord is the fulfillment of the best of humanity as he beckons us into the divine spirit. Jesus announces that he is the fulfillment of the Law and the Prophets. In other words, Jesus claims that the goal of Scripture is found in him. Certainly God recognized the magnificence of His Son. At his baptism, the Holy Spirit rests upon Jesus in the form of a dove, and the voice of the heavenly Father comes from on high, "You are my beloved Son, in you I am well pleased"

What if each night before we drifted off to sleep, we could hear a similar voice? Then those collective affirmations would form the pinnacle announcement, "Welcome home. In you I am well pleased." Today remind yourself that you, too, are God's beloved. How would your day be different if you really embraced this promise? No doubt a little more hopeful, less competitive and more confident of your infinite value.

Forgiveness: Letting Go of Your Own Suffering

OF ALL THE EXTRAORDINARY EVENTS in the life of John Paul II, few can compare with the 21 minutes he spent in a white-walled cell in Rome's Rebibia prison. Just after Christmas, 1983, the pope visited Mehmet Ali Agca, the man who 30 months earlier had shot him in St. Peter's Square. He presented Agca with a silver rosary and something else as well: his forgiveness.

While persistent unforgiveness is part of human nature, it works to the detriment not just of our spiritual well-being but our physical health as well. Holding onto anger has physiologic consequences—such as increased blood pressure and hormonal changes—linked to cardiovascular disease, immune suppression and, possibly, impaired neurological function and memory.

We can learn a lesson from nature. A rattlesnake, if cornered, will sometimes become so angry it will bite itself –exactly what happens when we harbor hate and resentment— we bring injury to ourselves. Or as comedian Buddy Hackett once confessed, "I've had a few arguments with people, but I never carry a grudge. You know why? While you're carrying a grudge, they're out dancing."

Forgiveness is really about letting go of our own suffering. Confucius no doubt understood this. He cautioned, "If you devote your life to seeking revenge, first dig two graves." Forgiveness does not mean you agree with what the other person did to you. It does not mean you can change what happened or erase what they did. What's done is done. All you can do is release yourself. Forgiveness is not something you do for someone else. It is a gift to yourself.

No wonder Jesus urges us to forgive "seventy-seven times." Begin by forgiving yourself; accept God's mercy and ask for protection against the venom of unforgiveness.

"More Than Anything Else, I Want This For My Son."

IT WAS A NOTRE DAME SUMMER EVENING: moms and dads, teenagers, little brothers and sisters all had gathered before the marble alter at the Grotto. They had come to campus for the Alumni Association Family Volunteer Camp. A feeling of uncertainty hung in the air as prayers and hymns united with the flickering candles. A few moms and dads wondered how their children would respond to people different from themselves – children and adults who held their bodies in awkward ways and showed an enthusiasm unlike the laughter and suave joking of their kid's friends. Parents wondered, "Will my kids work hard in the grueling sun – pulling weeds, shoveling gravel, chipping away wearied paint. Crabby teenagers can be a hazard in building family spirit. Will the kids embrace this notion of service and not resent our non-luxurious "vacation"?

It was the middle of the week when a dad revealed an amazing insight to a friend. "I used to think I'd give anything for my son to go to Notre Dame. I've found something even more important than that. I want David to have a compassionate heart. More than anything else, I want this for my son."

It's so easy to be deluded like the mother of James and John in the Gospel readng: "Declare that these two sons of mine will sit, one at your right hand and one at your left, in your kingdom." Naturally we want the best for our children. We may want our kids to be recognized athletes, to score the coveted 1400 SAT, to get the lead in the play. And on and on. While these accomplishments are indeed extraordinary, they become shallow and inconsequential when separated from the essence of greatness. Live your life so that when they think of greatness, they remember your compassion.

Take a Seat: Heaven or Hell?

A HOLY MAN WAS HAVING a conversation with the Lord one day and said, "Lord, I would like to know what Heaven and Hell are like." The Lord led the holy man to two doors. He opened one of the doors and the holy man looked in. In the middle of the room was a large round table. In the middle of the table was a large pot of stew which smelled delicious and made the holy man's mouth water.

But the people sitting around the table were thin and sickly. They were holding spoons with very long handles that were strapped to their arms and each found it possible to reach into the pot of stew and take a spoonful, but because the handle was longer than their arms, they could not get the spoons back into their mouths. The holy man shuddered at the sight of their misery and suffering. The Lord said, 'You have seen Hell.'

They then went to the next room and opened the door. It was exactly the same as the first one. There was the large round table with the large pot of stew which made the holy man's mouth water. The people were equipped with the same long-handled spoons, but here the people were well nourished and plump, laughing and talking. The holy man said, "I don't understand." "It is simple" said the Lord, "In this place the people have learned to feed one another." (author unknown)

Those who had learned to feed one another realized the importance of both receiving and giving. Sometimes we can struggle more with receiving than giving. To receive one must acknowledge need – a vulnerability that gifts the giver with importance and value. To always have it "all together" builds a distance, an aloofness with those who care the most for us. Relationships need authenticity that allows the removal of certitude's mask. You can only get so close to someone who fronts that image of the always capable spouse, colleague, or friend.

Our story depicts heaven as a place where everyone had something to give; there was no division created by earthly achievement. A culture of mutual benefit filled the room. But in hell no one gave and no one received. Such was the plight of the famous rich man that Jesus spoke of to his apostles. "Father Abraham, have mercy on me, and send Lazarus to dip the tip of his finger in water and cool my tongue; for I am in agony in these flames." But it was too late for the rich man—hell would be his eternal home. Today let your love

Heartbreak

No treachery is worse than betrayal by a family member or friend. Julius Caesar knew such treachery. Among the conspirators who assassinated the Roman leader on March 15, 44 B. C. was Marcus Junius Brutus. Caesar not only trusted Brutus, he had favored him as a son. According to Roman historians, Caesar first resisted the onslaught of the assassins. But when he saw Brutus among them with his dagger drawn, Caesar ceased to struggle and, pulling the top part of his robe over his face, asked the famous question, "You too, Brutus?"

Have you ever trusted someone whom you thought would give you truthful counsel, act on your behalf, or stand up for you when the pressure heated up? Instead of being your advocate, your guardian transformed into a Marcus Junius Brutus. At times like this, disillusionment can overwhelm us and betrayal can crush our spirits.

Jesus knew that "false prophets" would try to lead us away from him – deceive us with the appearance of goodness and the promise of something better. St. Paul was "convinced that neither death, nor life, nor angels, nor rulers, nor things present, nor things to come, nor powers, nor height, nor depth, nor anything else in all creation, will be able to separate us from the love of God in Christ Jesus our Lord." This day be comforted that our Good Shepherd can never be outdone in his faithfulness and generosity. Ask for his protection from any one or any thing that does not hold your best interest at heart.

A Mother's Love

THE YOUNG MOTHER SET HER foot on the path of life. "Is this the long way?" she asked. And the guide said: "Yes, and the way is hard. And you will be old before you reach the end of it. But the end will be better than the beginning." But the young mother was happy, and she would not believe that anything could be better than playing with her children, and gathering flowers for them along the way, and bathing them in the clear streams. Then the night came, and the storm, and the path was dark, and the children shook with fear and cold, and the mother drew them close and covered them with her mantle, and the children said, "Mother, we are not afraid, for you are near, and no harm can come."

And the morning came, and there was a hill ahead, and the children climbed and grew weary, and the mother was weary. But at all times she said to the children," A little patience and we are there." So the children climbed, and when they reached the top they said, "Mother, we would not have done it without you." And the mother, when she lay down at night looked up at the stars and said "This is a better day than the last, for my children have learned fortitude in the face of hardness. Yesterday I gave them courage. Today, I have given them strength."

And the next day came strange clouds which darkened the earth, clouds of war and hate and evil, and the children groped and stumbled, and the mother said: "Look up. Lift your eyes to the light." And the children looked and saw above the clouds an everlasting glory, and it guided them beyond the darkness. And that night the Mother said, "This is the best day of all, for I have shown my children God."

And the days went on, and the weeks and the months and the years, and the mother grew old and she was little and bent. But her children were tall and strong, and walked with courage. And when the way was rough, they lifted her for she was as light as a feather; and at last they came to a hill, and beyond they could see a shining road and golden gates flung wide. And mother said: "I have reached the end of my journey. And now I know the end is better than the beginning, for my children can walk alone, and their children after them."

And the children said, "You will always walk with us, Mother, even when you have gone through the gates." And they stood and watched her as she went on alone, and the gates closed after her. And they said: "We cannot see her, but she is with us still. A Mother like ours is more than a memory. Her love is eternal." (author unknown)

If you feel a few tears welling up inside, you know the power of loss and love – of a love that transcends life itself. Jesus tells us "My mother and my brothers are those who hear the word of God and do it." It's almost incomprehensible—the Creator of the Universe loves you even more than the unconditional love of parent for child.

In the Scriptures the crowd tells Jesus that his mother and relatives are looking for him. We might expect Jesus to immediately move the crowd aside so his Mother and his extended family could be near him. No doubt, he found them in a hurry. But first Jesus revealed a secret of the universe. The total dedication, the total love he felt so profoundly for Mary – he feels for you. As we follow day by day, that love penetrates through the inevitable sadness and haunting questions. We learn to focus on what we have left, not on what we have lost. Gratitude triumphs over scarcity.

"Follow me this day," Jesus begs us. Think a moment. Perhaps we need a new way of thinking toward another, toward a situation, toward all that we have. Maybe someone needs to hear from you; perhaps an apology is in order; maybe you just need to give yourself permission to laugh; to do something good for yourself—maybe to even acknowledge all that you have done right. Receive his love and pass it on today!

The Merciful Secret

DANIELLE HAD PROMISED her mom she would do better in school. Sometimes she forgot her homework, lost her place during reading class, and didn't finish the test. On this particular day, her teacher became perturbed with the students. It seemed everyone needed to be excused to visit the bathroom. But Danielle really had a legitimate excuse – but she had promised her mom she would not get on the teacher's bad side. Then the unforgivable happened. There sat Danielle in a puddle. Embarrassment and panic held her heart hostage. At that same moment, Hannah, was carrying a fish bowl past Danielle. Catching sight of Danielle's predicament, she chose to spill the fish water over the girl. The rest of the class rushed over to help Danielle and berated Hannah for her clumsiness. Hannah never revealed Danielle's secret. And Danielle remembered Hannah's mercy and generosity her whole life.

What a beautiful example of living Christ's request to his disciples: "Be merciful, just as your Father is merciful." Here are a few thoughts to ponder:

If you want to be miserable, then be merciless. Mercy prods. Often you have to confront someone about their thinking or behavior to help them become aware of the harm encircling that person.

Judgmental thinking is the product of lazy thinking. Enough negative thoughts can downsize your sense of well-being.

Judgmental comments are authoritative; they pronounce what is right and wrong, what should and should not be, what is valuable and what is worthless. Making a simple judgment, however, does not carry superior overtones. "Bill is overweight" is a judgment. That "Bill is slob who's going to break his chair" is judgmental.

It is so easy to conceal from ourselves the real motivation for judging another. Too often we judge out of our own insecurities –judging that is rooted in a wobbly self-worth. Sometimes it's just easier to be critical rather than to be constructive.

This day before you judge another ask this most important question: "What is my intent?" If your intent originates from love, for the higher good of others, to inspire justice, then grace paves your way; otherwise think twice before you speak or act.

St. Augustine had a large and beautiful table in his dining room where he invited needy people to dine. Engraved on the top of the table were these words: "Whoever loves another's name to blast, this table's not for him; so let him fast" Today let's feast. For we can trust that "A good measure, pressed down, shaken together, running over, will be put into your lap; for the measure you give will be the measure you get back."

It Really Is All About Love

A YOUNG MAN SAID to his father at breakfast one morning, "Dad, I'm going to get married." "How do you know you're ready to get married?" asked the father. "Are you in love?" "I sure am," said the son. "How do you know you're in love?" asked the father. "Last night as I was kissing my girlfriend good-night, her dog bit me and I didn't feel the pain until I got home." (author unknown)

Love – it really is all about love, isn't it! Perhaps you are praying for God to intervene with his love in your life. No matter how wise or how spiritual, no one can interpret the ways of God. We can not explain why one miracle and not another, why an apparent intervention here and not there. In all our prayers, whether we get the answers we want or not, we can trust in this one fact: God can make use of whatever happens. He tells us, "how much more will your Father in heaven give good things to those who ask him!" Pray with all your heart, trust in the Lord's generosity, and into His hands commend your spirit.

Find Something Beautiful
to Notice

SEVERAL YEARS AGO, a very special high school teacher lost her husband to a sudden heart attack. About a week after his death, she shared her insights with her students. "Before class is over, I would like to share with all of you a thought that is not related to class, but which I feel is very important. Each of us is put here on earth to learn, share, love, appreciate and give of ourselves. None of us knows when this fantastic experience will end. It can be taken away at any moment. Perhaps this is God's way of telling us that we must make the most out of every single day.

"So I would like you all to make me a promise. From now on, on your way to school, or on your way home, find something beautiful to notice. It doesn't have to be something you see — it could be a scent — perhaps of freshly baked bread wafting out of someone's house, or it could be the sound of the breeze slightly rustling the leaves in the trees, or the way the morning light catches one autumn leaf as it falls gently to the ground. Please look for these things, and cherish them. For, although it may sound trite to some, these things are the 'stuff' of life" The students picked up their books and filed out of the room silently. That afternoon, many of those students noticed more things on their way home from school than they had that whole semester. (source unknown)

Take notice of something special you experience today. Embrace that sign as a love note from Jesus to you. For he promises that "just as Jonah became a sign to the people of Nineveh, so the Son of Man will be to this generation." Ask to grow more sensitive, more appreciative of the numerous "miracles" that grace your life day by day. As we get older, it is not the things we did that we often regret, but the things we didn't do – that we bypassed from routine or self-preoccupation. May this day be filled with miracles for you!

The Grotto:
Where God Leaves a Message

ON FEBRUARY 11, 1858 BERNADETTE, her sister Toinette and a friend of theirs, Jeanne, went looking for wood in front of the Grotto of Massabielle in Lourdes, France. Bernadette heard a noise like a gust of wind, but none of the trees were moving. Raising her head, she saw in a hollow of the rock a small young lady, who smiled at her. This was the first Apparition of the Virgin Mary in Lourdes, France.

At the time of Bernadette, the Grotto was a dirty, hidden, and cold place. It was called the "pigs' shelter" because the pigs fed in the area and took shelter there. But it was here that the Virgin Mary, dressed in white, a sign of total purity, the sign of the Love of God – deigned to appear. What a contrast between this damp and obscure Grotto and the presence of the Virgin Mary, "the Immaculate Conception". It reminds us of the Gospel message – the meeting of the wealth of the goodness of God and the poverty of the human person.

God comes to join us where we are in the midst of our poverty and failures. The Grotto is not only a place where something happened – a geographical place – it is also a place where God gives us a sign by revealing his heart and our heart. Like the Grotto at Lourdes, our Notre Dame Grotto is a place where God leaves us a message – that He loves us as we are with all our successes but also with all our wounds, our weaknesses and our limitations.

Let us recall our affection for the Grotto by living out our Lord's challenge to us – a challenge that holds the key to our eternal life: "for I was hungry and you gave me food, I was thirsty and you gave me something to drink, I was a stranger and you welcomed me, I was naked and you gave me clothing, I was sick and you took care of me, I was in prison and you visited me."

Satan's Garage Sale

ONCE UPON A TIME, Satan was having a garage sale. He had tools that made it easy to tear others down; there were lenses for magnifying one's own importance and for diminishing others. Against the wall was the usual assortment of gardening implements guaranteed to help one's pride grow – the rake of scorn, the shovel of jealousy for digging a pit for one's neighbor and the tools of gossip, self-ishness and apathy. All the tools were attractively constructed and came complete with guarantees of prosperity. Prices, of course, were steep; but not to worry! Free credit was extended to one and all. "Take it home, use it and you won't have to pay until later!" old Satan called out , as he hawked his wares.

A visitor would also notice two well worn, non-descript tools standing in one corner. People often questioned why these items were higher priced than the others. They certainly appeared older and even a bit tattered. Satan would just laugh and answer, "Well, that's because I use them so much. If they weren't so plain looking, people might see them for what they were." Satan pointed to the two tools, saying, "You see, that one's Doubt and that one's Discouragement— and those will work when nothing else will." (author unknown)

Doubt and Discouragement – indeed powerful tools to bury us in anxiety, to weigh us down with feelings of helplessness – to place us on the desert with only the blistering sun as our guide and nour-ishment. In the dramatic gospel account of the man tortured by a legion of demons, we are touched by the mercy of our Lord. For years this tortured man had lived in the putrid tombs——small caves in the side of a hill. In his misery he had cried out day and night and ripped at his flesh with stones. With the authority of love, Jesus freed the man and restored his hope.

But this was not the outcome for the owners of the 2000 swine. In minutes their livelihood was brutally wiped out. "And the unclean spirits came out and entered the swine; and the herd, numbering about two thousand, rushed down the steep bank into the lake, and were drowned in the lake." Shocked, angered, and afraid these men "begged him to leave their neighborhood." Who wouldn't be distraught with the bizarre destruction of one's livelihood? Yet, like us, these men, lost all perspective. The moment's tragedy precluded them from recalling God's faithfulness in the past and his promise to love them into the future. Doubt and discouragement narrowed their memory; they forgot God's faithfulness and allowed the moment to become their despairing destiny.

Today pray for perspective. Our Lord who delivered you from previous difficulties is the same loving God who so desires your peace and fulfillment. Hold to this thought and walk step by step confident that good times will return.

The Rocking Chair

THERE WAS ONCE AN ELDERLY, despondent woman in a nursing home. She wouldn't speak to anyone or request anything. She merely existed – rocking in her creaky old rocking chair. The old woman didn't have many visitors. But every couple mornings, a concerned and wise young nurse would go into her room. She didn't try to speak or ask questions of the old lady. She simply pulled up another rocking chair beside the old woman and rocked with her. Weeks or months later, the old woman finally spoke. 'Thank you,' she said. 'Thank you for rocking with me.'" (author unknown)

Do you think the nurse ever thought, "I'm really not up to this today?" or "Am I just wasting my time with someone who doesn't even know or care that I'm here?" Probably. But she kept on rocking. Why? Because Christ needed her to be his presence in that chair. The old woman needed to know that she mattered; that she was important to someone. And what about you? Is something tugging at you? Is there a rocking chair waiting for you? Trust in his words. "For those who want to save their life will lose it, and those who lose their life for my sake will save it."

The Girl with the Rose

<hr />

JOHN BLANCHARD STOOD UP from the bench, straightened his Army uniform, and studied the crowd of people making their way through Grand Central Station. He looked for the girl whose heart he knew, but whose face he didn't – the girl with the rose. His interest in her had begun thirteen months before in a Florida library. Taking a book off the shelf he found himself intrigued, not with the words of the book, but with the notes penciled in the margin.

The soft handwriting reflected a thoughtful soul and insightful mind. In the front of the book, he discovered the previous owner's name, Miss Hollis Maynell. With time and effort he located her address. He wrote her a letter introducing himself and invited her to correspond. The next day he was shipped overseas for service in World War II. During the next year and one month, the two grew to know each other through the mail. Each letter was a seed falling on a fertile heart. Blanchard requested a photograph, but she refused. She felt that if he really cared, it wouldn't matter what she looked like. When the day finally came for him to return from Europe, they scheduled their first meeting – 7:00 p.m. at the Grand Central Station in New York. "You'll recognize me," she wrote, "by the red rose I'll be wearing on my lapel." So at 7:00p.m. he was in the station looking for a girl whose heart he loved, but whose face he'd never seen.

Blanchard noticed a very attractive young woman who also noticed him. "Going my way, sailor?" she murmured. He made one step closer to her, and then saw Hollis Maynell. A woman well past 40, she was more than plump, her thick-ankled feet thrust into low-heeled shoes. The girl in the green suit was walking quickly away. Blanchard felt as though he was split in two – so keen was his desire to follow her, and yet so deep was his longing for the woman whose spirit had truly companioned him and upheld his own.

And there she stood. He did not hesitate. His fingers gripped the small worn blue leather copy of the book that was to identify him to her. This would not be love, but it would be something precious, something perhaps even better than love, a friendship for which he had been and must ever be grateful. Mr. Blanchard squared his shoulders, saluted and held out the book to the woman—yet as he spoke he felt choked by the bitterness of his disappointment.

"I'm Lieutenant John Blanchard, and you must be Miss Maynell. The woman's face broadened into a tolerant smile. "I don't know what this is about, son," she answered, "but the young lady in the green suit who just went by, begged me to wear this rose on my coat. I am to tell you that she is waiting for you in the big restaurant across the street. She said it was some kind of test!" Much was revealed that day about Mr. Blanchard. His choice clearly revealed the depth of his character. "Tell me whom you love," Houssaye wrote, "And I will tell you who you are..." (author unknown)

What does our Lord's love tell us about Him and about us? Like his apostles, we, too, "are to preach the good news to all creation." What is this good news? For many of us, the good news is simply too good to fully embrace. The Son of God, the creator of the universe, thinks you are irreplaceable. He gave his life so you could have life eternal. Can you preach the good news through what you say and don't say – in your decision making, in the routine occasions – car-pooling, cooking, cleaning, staff meetings, athletic events? This day trust in his continuous devotion to you; move in the direction of the Spirit's prompting and be open to the surprises that await you!

House of 1000 Mirrors

LONG AGO IN A SMALL, far away village, there was place known as the House of 1000 Mirrors. A small, happy little dog learned of this place and decided to visit. When he arrived, he looked through the doorway with his ears lifted high and his tail wagging as fast as it could. To his great surprise, he found himself staring at 1000 other happy little dogs with their tails wagging just as fast as his. When he left the House, he thought to himself, "This is a wonderful place. I will come back and visit it often."

In this same village, another little dog, who was not quite as happy as the first one, decided to visit the house. He slowly climbed the stairs and hung his head low as he looked into the door. When he saw the 1000 unfriendly looking dogs staring back at him, he growled at them and was horrified to see 1000 little dogs growling back at him. As he left, he thought to himself, "That is a horrible place, and I will never go back there again."

If a critic of Jesus visited the House of 1000 Mirrors, growling dogs would certainly surround the person. Such an individual would seek out others like himself – looking for opportunities to denounce Jesus and his followers. In the Gospel we hear Jesus' character questioned: "Why do John's disciples and the disciples of the Pharisees fast, but your disciples do not fast?" What motivated such a comment? Jealousy? Ignorance? Rigidity that blinds against the bigger principle?

There may be days when the growl controls our voice. Something hollow within moves us to tear down – to look for the shortcomings of others. At other times we are the recipient of such jealousy, of other's greed, insensitivity and self-preoccupation. Jesus explains "no one puts new wine into old wineskins; otherwise, the wine will burst the skins, and the wine is lost, and so are the skins; but one puts new wine into fresh wineskins." In the whole world only you will meet the sequence of people who will cross your path today. You are the body of Christ – new wine in fresh wineskin.

Through patience with yourself and others, by way of attentive presence and truthfilled conversation – you are His voice, His touch, His eyes. Nothing ordinary about today – you will be Christ to many. If you come upon the House of 1000 Mirrors, be sure to say "hi" to the dogs with wagging tales.

The Mustard Seed: Our Destiny

A NOTED BRAIN SURGEON, Dr. Bronson Ray, was taking a stroll when he saw a boy on a scooter smash headfirst into a tree. Realizing that the boy was seriously injured, the doctor told a bystander to call an ambulance. As he proceeded to administer first aid, a boy not much older than the injured one nudged through the crowd that had gathered and said to Dr. Ray, "I'd better take over now, sir. I'm a Boy Scout and I know first aid."

That Boy Scout reminds us of the mustard seed in the parable told by Jesus—small but ever so mighty in potential. Did you know that the mustard seed is a plant of tremendous growth? Though it appears the smallest of all seeds, its destiny is greatness. This seed will grow up to 15 feet tall! In the parable the sower knew exactly where to toss the seed so its life could fully develop. In the divine scheme of things, the mustard seed would flourish for a particular purpose – to serve. It's very common for birds to seek its treelike bush for shelter and companionship.

Do you ever doubt your potential to lead an extraordinary life? Ever feel a bit insignificant? Remember who sowed you; he knew exactly which gifts you needed – and did not need – to build his kingdom. Today guard against comparing yourself to others. You cannot control if someone is more intelligent, better looking, wealthier, more athletic, etc. You can, however, control doing your best. Keep the faith. The mustard seed is destined for greatness. Someone needs you to keep on growing!

The Surprise Announcement

ONCE THERE WAS AN EMPEROR in the Far East who was growing old and knew it was time to choose his successor. "It has come time for me to step down and to choose the next emperor. I am going to give each of you a seed today that I want you to grow. I will then judge the plants that you bring to me, and the one I choose will be the next emperor of the kingdom!"

A boy named Ling received a seed, but he simply could not get the seed to grow. Six months went by, still nothing in Ling's pot. He just knew he had killed his seed. A year finally went by and all the youths of the kingdom brought their plants to the emperor for inspection. When the emperor arrived, he surveyed the room and greeted the young people. "My, what great plants, trees and flowers you have grown," said the emperor.

All of a sudden, the emperor spotted Ling at the back of the room with his empty pot. He ordered his guards to bring him to the front. "Behold your new emperor! His name is Ling!" Ling couldn't believe it. How could he be the new emperor? Then the emperor said, "One year ago today, I gave everyone here a seed. I told you to take the seed, plant it, water it, and bring it back to me today. But I gave you all boiled seeds which would not grow.

All of you, except Ling, have brought me trees and plants and flowers. When you found that the seed would not grow, you substituted another seed for the one I gave you. Ling was the only one with the courage and honesty to bring me a pot with my seed in it. Therefore, he is the one who will be the new emperor!"

Those competing for the throne resemble the people Jesus speaks of in his parable about the seeds. "And others are those sown among the thorns: these are the ones who hear the word, but the cares of the world, and the lure of wealth, and the desire for other things come in and choke the word, and it yields nothing." Sometimes the cares of the world cause us to pull within and become more and more preoccupied with ourselves. Self-absorption causes us to lose perspective, to just go about our usual chores, and to overlook the positives all around us.

Jesus wants us to claim his promise that those who "hear the word and accept it." will "bear fruit, thirty and sixty and a hundredfold." Today let's be mindful of one thing that tries to restrict our celebration of Christ's presence. Ask our Lord to bring clarity and strength to you; ask for patience and promptings to think and act with his divine assurance. And don't forget to trust his word: you will "bear fruit, thirty and sixty and a hundredfold."

Be Mindful of Your Motives

"THE MAN WHO SINGS his own praises is usually off key."

Toward the beginning of the third century B.C, the king of Egypt ordered Sostratos, a renowned architect, was asked to build the famous beacon light of Alexandria. This structure would guide the ships safely to the port. When the building was completed, Sostratos chiseled his own name on the grand edifice. Not wanting his name to be readily visible, he covered it with mud and whitewash. On top of this he wrote the king's name with gold letters. When the waves hit the mud it would eventually wash away the sovereign's name and the architect's name would triumph.

The hypocrisy of Sostratos reminds us of the Pharisees that Jesus chastises in the Gospel. They use God to promote themselves; they manipulate and abuse sacred practices to secure worldly praise and honor. "Beware of practicing your piety before others in order to be seen by them; for then you have no reward from your Father in heaven." There is a fine line between prudently sharing our successes with others and letting success drive our motive and behavior. If our spiritual practices focus on uniting our will with God's and on celebrating his love for us, then our behavior at work and home should be the fruit of our prayer. Today be mindful of your motives driving your actions – even actions that appear quite admirable to others. If you sincerely pray that all you do be for God's purpose and his honor, then you will travel with a joyful integrity.

Just the First Step;
Not the Whole Staircase

A GROUP OF EXPECTANT FATHERS were in a waiting room, while their wives were in the process of delivering babies. A nurse came in and announced to one man that his wife had just given birth to twins. "That's quite a coincidence" he responded, "I play for the Minnesota Twins!" A few minutes later another nurse came in and announced to another man that he was the father of triplets. "That's amazing," he exclaimed, "I work for the 3M company." At that point, a third man slipped off his chair and lay down on the floor. Somebody asked him if he was feeling ill. "No," he responded, "I happen to work for the 7-up company." (author unknown)

Parenting brings the greatest joys and sometimes the greatest heart-aches. Most parents agree that the loss of child would agonize their soul more than any other life adversity. In the scriptures we meet a powerful official whose son is dying. We can understand the man's plea to Jesus. "….he begged him to come down and heal his son, for he was at the point of death" Jesus challenges the man's faith. Our Lord will not go to the gravely ill boy; instead he promises to heal from afar. Jesus tells the man, "Go; your son will live." And the father trusts the Lord and begins to make his way back home.

Perhaps the father thought to himself, "That's great. I do believe you. But just in case why don't you come with me." Nonetheless, the father trusts, walks with patience, and hears the most wonderful news from his slave. "Yesterday at one in the afternoon the fever left him." The father realized that this was the hour when Jesus had said to him, "Your son will live." This father teaches us that we need to take the first step in faith. We don't need to see the whole staircase; we just need to take the first step. Recognize the various people who reach out to you and your child – people who listen, guide, encourage, and even ask you to practice tough love. Trust in them and the one who sent them.

God Writes Straight with Crooked Lines

DEATH WAS WALKING toward a city one morning and a man asked, "What are you going to do?"

"I'm going to take 100 people," Death replied.

"That's horrible!" the man said.

"That's the way it is," Death said. "That's what I do."

The man hurried to warn everyone he could about Death's plan.

As evening fell, he met Death again. "You told me you were going to take 100 people," the man said. "Why did 1,000 die?"

"I kept my word," Death responded. "I only took 100 people. Worry took the others." (author unknown)

Ask any parent if worry ever knocked upon the door of parenting. It seems inevitable, if you love then worry will be your aching companion. Jesus understands the love of parent for child. He also desperately wants to ease our worry by walking our path with us – not just a few days of the week, but every single day and every single minute. If we look to the gospel, we meet a father who pleads for Jesus to save his daughter's life. Hope appears short lived. For while this father waits for Jesus to leave the crowd, the horrific news arrives: 'Your daughter is dead. Why trouble the teacher any further?' Hearing this announcement, Jesus says to the father, 'Do not fear, only believe.' The man's daughter is brought back to life – the ultimate agony for any parent has been avoided.

What exactly does it mean to "not fear, only believe"? Loss is an inevitable part of life. No matter how much one believes, jobs will be lost, people will break our hearts, disease will limit our lives, and death will steal away those we love. How then does one "not fear, only believe"? Fear not that you are alone in your sadness; believe that our Lord cries with you and will walk you through the valley of grief and emptiness. And in the grand scheme of your life remember that "God writes straight with crooked lines."

The Meaning of Life
in Five Words

A PROFESSIONAL GOLFER had a few words with his caddy known for his talkative personality. Before teeing off, the golfer explained, "Don't say a word to me. And if I ask you something, just answer yes or no." During the round, the golfer found the ball next to a tree. The shot required that the ball be hit under a branch, over a lake and onto the green. Sizing up the shot, the golfer asked the caddy, "Five-iron?"

"No," the caddy said.

"What do you mean, not a five-iron?" snorted the golfer. "Watch this shot."

The caddy rolled his eyes. "No-o-o. "

The golfer hit the ball, and it stopped two feet from the hole. He turned to his caddy, handed him the five-iron and said, "Now what do you think about that? You can talk now."

The caddy answered, "That wasn't your ball." *(Bits and Pieces)*

It is so easy to get confused when we focus only on doing the "rite" things rather the "right" things. In scripture Jesus defends his disciples when the Pharisees accuse them of breaking the law. "One sabbath he was going through the grainfields; and as they made their way his disciples began to pluck heads of grain. The Pharisees said to him, "Look, why are they doing what is not lawful on the sabbath?"" And Jesus replied, "The sabbath was made for humankind, and not humankind for the sabbath; so the Son of Man is lord even of the sabbath."

An important person in the history of Judaism was a man named Hillel. When asked if it was possible to stand on one leg and teach the whole of the Torah – known for its countless laws – Hillel obliged. He smiled, lifted one leg off the ground and said, "Love your neighbor as yourself. Everything else is commentary."

Rules, rituals, and religious traditions are not ends in themselves but are means to an end. What God wants is a relationship with his people marked by trust and love. Go forth this day and remember you have a part to play. There's no stand in for you. Don't be concerned. You have the best director of all eternity coaching you scene by scene!

Stay True

A SCOTTISH PREACHER named Andrew Bonar wrote a diary entry that acknowledged his struggle with envy. "This day 20 years ago I preached for the first time as an ordained minister. It is amazing that the Lord has spared me and used me at all. I have no reason to wonder that He used others far more than He does me. Yet envy is my hurt, and today I have been seeking grace to rejoice exceedingly over the usefulness of others, even where it cast me into the shade. Lord, take away this envy from me!"

Such envy plagued the Pharisees who sought to destroy the reputation of Jesus. If only they could stop the people from crowding around Jesus; if only they could ruin his name and turn the adulation back upon themselves. The Pharisees had raised concerns about Jesus even amongst his cousin's followers. When the disciples of John came to Jesus, they asked, "Why do we and the Pharisees fast often, but your disciples do not fast?" Though some might have been apologetic to the Pharisees or tried to assuage the accusations of John's disciples, Jesus refused to submit to their pressure. He responded, "The wedding guests cannot mourn as long as the bridegroom is with them, can they? The days will come when the bridegroom is taken away from them, and then they will fast."

As we move through our day, don't let judgmental remarks steal away your resolve to do right. Don't be surprised by the petty comments. And most of all do not hand over your happiness to people who thrive on casting doubt on the good work of others. Trust yourself. Pray with sincerity. And believe in the power of your mission.

Chained Like the Elephant?

DURING A TOUR OF THE Ringling Brothers Barnum & Bailey Circus, a man noticed that the elephants were being held by only a small rope tied to their front leg. No chains, no cages. The elephants could, at any time, break away from their bonds but for some reason, they did not. The trainer explained "when they are very young and much smaller we use the same size rope to tie them and, at that age, it's enough to hold them. As they grow up, they are conditioned to believe they cannot break away. They think the rope can still hold them, so they never try to break free." (author unknown)

Sometimes we cultivate beliefs that limit our fullness of life. How often do we sigh, "I just don't have time to take care of myself?" Too many demands coming at me – work, family, kids." Jesus must have had similar thoughts. Imagine the desperation of those carrying their beloved sick to him. So many people to cure – everyone begging him to end their suffering. Yet Jesus pulls himself away from the crowd. "At daybreak he departed and went into a deserted place."

Even Jesus needed a moment of respite; time to renew himself – body and spirit. Had Jesus forfeited this time to himself, he might have cured dozens and dozens of people. Did he make the right decision? Absolutely. Everything good in life follows the laws of balance. Perhaps Mother Teresa said it best: "If you want to keep the lamp burning, you need to keep putting oil in it." Maybe your life is similar to the elephant's. You remain chained by the thought – life is just too busy for me to take care of myself. Give yourself permission to invest in yourself. Jesus wants this for us. We do no one any good if we deplete our health, our energy, our enthusiasm for life. Enjoy the day and know that the old rope holding you back is just an illusion. And if you like chocolate chip ice cream, stop by the ice cream shop today.

Influence: Christ-Like Authority

A PASTOR ON THE VERGE of a breakdown was urged to see the psychiatrist Carl Jung. When asked how many hours a day he was working, the pastor told Jung "about eighteen hours a day." Jung advised him to cut down to eight hours a day and spend time in quiet relaxation. The first day the pastor sat down in a comfortable armchair to listen to Mozart and read a novel. The second day he listened to Beethoven . . .and so on. After two weeks the pastor felt, if anything, worse and returned to Jung. The psychiatrist asked him how he was spending his time. When the pastor described his leisure hours, Jung said, "That is not what I meant; I want you to spend time quietly with yourself." The man replied, "I could not think of anything more appalling." Jung said, "Well, that is the person you have been inflicting on your people eighteen hours a day." (author unknown)

The pastor ran from self-knowledge and burdened his congregation with his ego driven motives. How different from Jesus. What must it have been like to hear our Lord preach? Was it how he looked into the eyes of his listeners? What did one hear in his voice? Truth without cynicism. Certitude without arrogance. Confidence because of a higher purpose—not conquest for higher praise. Sincerity not slogans. Jesus persevered despite constant attacks because he believed in his Father's faithfulness. Did he suffer feelings of abandonment? Did he pray with angst in his voice? Yes. But Jesus always remembered the promise – "You are my beloved Son."

People experienced Jesus' power precisely because he did not seek it. His authority resonated because he acted out of compassion while setting clear expectations for his followers. "They were astounded at his teaching, for he taught them as one having authority, and not as the scribes." On our own we cannot speak with an authority that is sturdy in its motive; we cannot sustain our fidelity to do right when loss threatens our personal and financial security. The good news – we aren't expected to do this on our own. Surrender your day to Him. Gather support from someone who loves you. Trust in God. Believe in yourself. And genuine authority will be yours!

Get Away from Your Work

"Every now and then go away, have a little relaxation, for when you come back to your work your judgment will be surer, since to remain constantly at work will cause you to lose power of judgment… Go some distance away because then the work appears smaller, and more of it can be taken in at a glance, and lack of harmony or proportion is more readily seen." These are the words of Leonardo da Vinci, and no idler he; he excelled as a painter, sculptor, poet, architect, engineer, city planner, scientist, inventor, anatomist, military genius, and philosopher.

Would Jesus agree with Leonardo da Vinic's philosophy? Imagine the crowds following Jesus. So much suffering – body's ravaged by disease – minds anguished by life's scars. Everybody desperate for their chance to find hope. Did Jesus become overwhelmed by the multitude that begged for his time and help? Did our Lord get worn down by all those needy people? Did he ever walk away from the desperate sufferer to renew himself? Yes! Jesus understood the importance of recharging his battery – of taking care of himself. We read in the Gospel: "But now more than ever the word about Jesus spread abroad; many crowds would gather to hear him and to be cured of their diseases. But he would withdraw to deserted places and pray"

Mother Teresa tells us, "If you want to keep the lamp burning, you need to keep putting oil in it." It's tough though to look after ourselves when those we love are hurting, drifting, or simply needing our attention. Jesus is our role model. If the Messiah took time to center himself, we must give ourselves permission to do the same. Do you need to spend more time with our Lord? Do you need to take time to eat better? Get more sleep? Exercise? Do something fun? Enjoy your spouse's company? Play with your kids? Visit with a friend? If we don't renew ourselves, we will sabotage our efforts to be there for others. Leonardo Da Vinci was right. "Every now and then go away, have a little relaxation, for when you come back to your work your judgment will be surer."

It's A Given

IN 1986 ANGRY FILIPINOS took to the streets of Manila and drove Ferdinand and Imelda Marcos from power. In her haste to escape into exile, Imelda left behind more than 1,200 pairs of shoes, 427 designer dresses, and 71 pairs of sunglasses. In a country where two out of every three households lacked adequate food, this was extravagant to say the least! During their twenty years in power, the couple plundered nearly $12 billion from their poverty-stricken country.

All of history had waited for the birth of the Messiah. Would he be the king of kings who would lay low the enemies of the Jewish people? Would he wield his power to satiate his own needs? Would egocentric personalities like that of the Marcos clan mark his kingship?

Jesus chooses a passage from Isaiah to announce his mission statement. In the synagogue he reads, "The Spirit of the Lord is upon me, because he has anointed me to bring good news to the poor. He has sent me to proclaim release to the captives and recovery of sight to the blind, to let the oppressed go free, to proclaim the year of the Lord's favor." When Jesus rolls up the scroll and hands it back to the attendant, all are transfixed by him. Then our Lord's magnificent announcement: "Today this scripture has been fulfilled in your hearing."

How do we know the Spirit directs our thoughts and actions? It's not difficult. Mother Teresa tells us that Jesus is found in the disguise of the poor, in the disguise of those suffering loneliness, in the disguise of those oppressed by mental and physical pain. Wouldn't it be magnificent if we went about our day knowing that "The Spirit of the Lord is upon me!" This is not a wish; this is a given. Claim it. Move through your day anointed by his Spirit.

God, Why Are You Sleeping?

FORTUNE TELLER, gazing into crystal ball, to frog: You are going to meet a beautiful young woman. From the moment she sets eyes on you she will have an insatiable desire to know all about you. She will be compelled to get close to you—you'll fascinate her."

Frog: "Where am I? At a singles club?"

Fortune teller: "Biology class." (author unknown)

Sometimes we feel like the frog. Doesn't our Lord promise us abundant life? Well, then why do find ourselves in topsy-turvy situations. Certainly Jesus' apostles had felt the same way. In one 24 hour period, they had participated in a miracle that fed 5000 people and then, before the next day's dawn, the apostles were battling the angry waves with their fatigued bodies. And where is Jesus ? Back on the shore – probably praying or sleeping. But it's not the raging waters that ultimately tortured the apostles; it's the perceived ghost walking on the water.

"But when they saw him walking on the sea, they thought it was a ghost and cried out; for they all saw him and were terrified. But immediately he spoke to them and said, "Take heart, it is I; do not be afraid." Then he got into the boat with them and the wind ceased. When storms threaten us, we cry out to God, "God, why are you sleeping?" Yet we hold to this hope: There is someone bigger than the storm and more powerful than the waters that threaten to overtake us. Today scoot over in your boat. Take a deep breath – rely on the power of your captain to bring you through the storm.